# SRI RAMANA MAHARSHI

## The Supreme Guru

Alan Jacobs

**YogiImpressions**®

**YogiImpressions**®

SRI RAMANA MAHARSHI
First published in India in 2010 by
**Yogi Impressions Books Pvt. Ltd.**
1711, Centre 1, World Trade Centre,
Cuffe Parade, Mumbai 400 005, India.
Website: www.yogiimpressions.com

First Edition: October 2010

Copyright © 2010 by Alan Jacobs

Cover concept and book design by Shiv Sharma.
Photos courtesy: Sri Ramanasramam Archival Centre, Tiruvannamalai.
Picture of Arunachala Hill on back cover by Benjamin Larrea.
Photo of Swami Ramdas courtesy Anandashram.
Photo of Sri Hariwansh Lal Poonja courtesy Avadhuta Foundation.

ISBN 978-81-88479-69-6

Printed at: Uchitha Graphic Printers Pvt. Ltd., Mumbai

# CONTENTS

*Two pilgrims pause for a rest on the holy mountain of Arunachala, to admire the breathtaking view of the temple town of Tiruvannamalai in the distance.*

*Sri Ramana Maharshi reclining on a couch in the old Hall of the ashram.*

# INTRODUCTION

Sri Bhagavan Ramana Maharshi is universally regarded as a great World Teacher and as the Supreme Guru. Tradition proclaims that every thousand or more years, a supreme guru, of the highest calibre, appears on this planet to set a new agenda for the coming millennium. This is Divine Grace, to assist all those perplexed men and women trapped in *samsara* – the endless cycle of suffering births and rebirths – and wishing to wake up and free themselves from this bondage.

The revered Adi Shankara was the last to fulfil this historic mission in the years between the 7th and 8th centuries AD. He clarified the eternal principles residing in the highest teaching of Advaita Vedanta which, when applied, leads to Self-realisation. In his commentaries on Sage Vyasa's *Brahma Sutras*, he lucidly codified the ancient

Non-dual Vedic and Upanishadic knowledge into a systematic form, easy for assimilation by the men and women of his day, and in the days to come. Now Bhagavan Sri Ramana Maharshi has appeared, upholding the teaching of Shankara, but bringing certain important innovations for this current millennium and the generations to come.

Primarily, the Maharshi has made the great science of Self-Enquiry or *Atma Vichara* easier and brought it into the open, making it readily available for all, and no longer kept as a secret to be revealed only to the initiated brahmin pupils of traditional gurus. Sri Bhagavan let his Teaching encompass the Western world, as well as Asia, as it naturally did, leading to his being recognised as a true *Jagadguru*, the World Teacher.

The Maharshi was able to transmit his *Jnana* of Non-dual, Self-knowledge through Silence – a rare spiritual power, following the precedent set by the divine primeval guru, Lord Dakshinamurti, who was deemed a manifestation of Lord Shiva. He could readily converse with birds and animals, a unique gift possessed by only a few saints.

He also lived an impeccable life without any trace of blemish on his noble character, and was a veritable ocean of love, devotion, wisdom and compassion to all who came into his orbit.

By his ineffable presence and Teaching, he created a global renaissance of interest in the high doctrines of Advaita Vedanta. He started a wild forest fire that is remorselessly burning down much of the dense forest of samsara, that is trapping humankind.

In this short and concise biography, I shall endeavour to portray his historic greatness and illustrate the tremendous advancements he has made towards the spiritual knowledge of mankind. At the same time, I will outline his important contribution towards the alleviation of the human condition on our troubled planet.

I also hope to, once again, make the fundamental principles of his great Teaching clear, for the benefit of those earnestly seeking the Truth about the nature of their real Self, and the apparent world in which we all live.

I have also included some poetry that is relevant to his great Teaching, an art that Sri Bhagavan himself loved, and in which he was a natural master.

— Alan Jacobs, President,
Ramana Maharshi Foundation, UK
London, January 2010

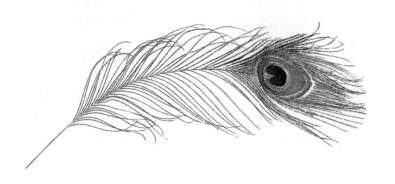

Chapter One

# FAMILY BACKGROUND

*"May Thou and I be one and inseparable like Alagu and Sundaram, O Arunachala!"*

– V. 2, The Marital Garland of Letters

The boy, later to become world famous as Sri Bhagavan Ramana Maharshi, was born into an ancient and revered brahmin family, one hour after midnight, on Monday, December 30, 1879, during *Ardra Darsanam* – the festival to celebrate Lord Shiva's cosmic dance as Natarajan. This has always been commemorated as a highly auspicious day when, according to the *Puranas* – a collection of ancient Hindu religious texts, Lord Shiva appeared before his favoured devotees Gautama and Patanjali. The strong, healthy child born to Sundaram and Alagu was named Venkataraman, after their family deity.

He was the second of three sons of Sundaram Iyer, a highly respected, well-to-do brahmin who was a Court Pleader in the temple town of Tiruchuzhi in Tamil Nadu. Sundaram's father was Nagaswami Iyer of the Gothram lineage, issuing from the sage Parasara, from which the great Rishi Vyasa was also descended. Nagaswami had four sons, Venkateswaran, Sundaram, Subbiah and Nelliappier, and a daughter named Lakshmi Ammal. The eldest son, Venkatesa, bore the family responsibility for some time after his father's death, but later became a renunciate. The second son, Sundaram, then bore the family responsibility.

Venkataraman's mother, who was later to reach great spiritual heights in her own right, was named Azhagammal. Both parents' names coincidently meant 'Beauty', his mother's in Tamil and his father's in Sanskrit. Tiruchuzhi is confirmed in the Puranas as a sacred place, where following three huge, threatening deluges, Lord Shiva miraculously intervened to save the town.

Venkataraman's mother and father were well known for their intense devotion to Lord Shiva. His mother knew many devotional songs, full of Advaitic truth, and was gifted with a delightfully melodious singing voice. From all that she has related about her son's birth, she said that during her

*Venkataraman's father Sundaram Iyer.*

*Venkataraman's mother Azhagammal.*

pregnancy she had experienced a most unusual pain in her abdomen. This was interpreted as being caused by the entry of a brilliant Being into her womb. At that time, she was said to have developed a wondrous lustre such as she had never displayed before. At the baby's birth, the midwife experienced a great blinding light. She told Azhagammal of her wonderful vision and said, "He who is born today in your house must be a Divine Being!" This event created much wonderment and speculation at the time: a prophecy that was to be perfectly fulfilled as the child grew up to adolescence and manhood.

He was brought up along with his elder brother Nagaswami, and Sundaram's deceased sister, Lakshmi Ammal's two children, Ramaswami and Meenakshi.

When Sundaram Iyer died prematurely in 1892, he left three sons and a daughter, Nagaswami aged fourteen, Venkataraman aged twelve, Nagasundaram aged six and a daughter Alamelu aged four. As our story unfolds, we shall see how this noble extended family played an important part in Venkataraman's remarkable and historic destiny.

# Chapter Two

# CHILDHOOD

*"In Thee, O Arunachala, all, having come into being and
having stayed for a while, attain resolution. This is wonderful.
In the heart, Thou dancest as 'I', as the Self. O Lord, they
call Thee by the name 'Heart'."*

– V. 2, Arunachala Pancharatnam

The young Venkataraman's childhood was as perfectly
normal as any childhood could be. He was a well-built,
robust lad, and had been breast-fed by his devoted mother
until he was five years old.

There was also a motherless cousin, Meenakshi, living
in the house at the same time. She was also breast-fed
by mother Azhagammal. It later transpired that young
Venkataraman gave comfort to his cousin Meenakshi at the

*The young Venkataraman attended the Sethupathi Elementary School in Tiruchuzhi.*

time of her unfortunate early death. The boy went near her and touched her. She rose up in surprise and said, "Who is it who has touched me?" This happened during the last moments of her life.

Young Venkataraman was exceptionally friendly and good natured, and was much loved by all the villagers. His open-mindedness, geniality and sense of humour were much admired. He attended the Sethupathi Elementary School in Tiruchuzhi for three years, where he learned the rudiments of Tamil, English and Arithmetic. As a young boy he had many playmates: one of his neighbour's children Chellam, and his sister Subbukutty, were his close friends. Their aunt was very fond of Venkataraman and he was often invited into their home. There was also a boy called Kathirvelu whose name the young Venkataraman inscribed in his notebook, which is still there for all to see.

When he was eleven years old, he moved to the secondary school in Dindigul where his elder brother Nagaswami was known to be a diligent student. Venkataraman, although intelligent, did not seem to take much pleasure in school work. He was more interested in playing football and other sports. There, in the spacious Bhuminatheshwara temple corridors and the green open spaces surrounding the

*The tank of Bhuminatheshwara temple where the young Venkataraman swam with his friends.*

temple shrine, he and his friends took frequent dips in the *soola thirtha* – the temple tank. He possessed a truly compassionate heart, and this is illustrated by the following story that he later recounted when he helped a neighbouring boy. "One day a boy, three years younger, took a sugar cane together with a knife. As he could not cut it himself, he asked his brothers to assist him but they ignored his request. I felt sorry for him. I took the sugar cane and tried to cut it. My finger was cut in the process and began to bleed. The boy began to weep so I managed to cut the cane into slices. I tied my finger with a wet cloth, the bleeding however, did not stop right away."

The rite of *Upanayama* or putting on the sacred brahmin

thread was performed when he was eight years old.

There was a family legend which now seems relevant to this account of his auspicious childhood. One day, long ago, a sadhu came to the ancestral house begging for food. Unfortunately, against tradition, he was not treated with the proper respect nor given a meal. The sadhu promptly issued a curse stating that from now on one member of each generation in this family would wander about, begging like himself. The 'curse' came true because in each generation one member renounced family life to become a wandering ascetic. One of Sundaram's uncles had donned an ochre robe, and his elder brother Venkatesa had also taken the same path. Little did Sundaram know that his son Venkataraman would also become a sadhu, but turn what was considered a 'curse' into a bountiful blessing for all humanity.

In 1892, the whole family suffered a grave shock. Sundaram, after a short illness, suddenly and without warning, died. He left behind three sons, his wife and a daughter. When the young Venkataraman returned from school to see his father lying dead, it made a tremendous impression upon him. He asked, "When Father is lying here, why do you say that he has gone?" This question must have been pondered upon considerably, as it was the question of death, to which he was later to return with amazing consequences.

This sudden demise led to the division of this close-knit family. Azhagammal moved to Manamadurai with her two younger children. The two elder children, including Venkataraman, were taken into the care of a kindly uncle, Subbiah Iyer, and moved to his house overlooking the magnificent Meenakshi temple in the town of Madurai.

Here, Venkataraman was sent to Scott's Middle School, and later on to the American Mission High School. He was an average pupil who learned easily but showed very little interest in the worldliness of the lessons. Later, he recounted

*Venkataraman studied at the American Mission High School in Madurai.*

his memories of this time. "While the school lessons were being taught, lest I should fall asleep, I used to tie a thread to a nail on the wall, and tie my hair to it. When the head nodded, the thread pulled tight and used to wake me up. Otherwise, the teacher would twist my ears."

He liked athletics and was stronger than most other boys of his age. He also enjoyed playing football, and people commented that somehow his team always managed to win, hence he earned the nickname of 'Tangakai' which means 'Golden Hand'. In his uncle's house at Madurai, a great change was soon to come over the lad who would influence the whole world for generations to come.

He was given a room on the top floor which was un-used. Here he would play 'throw ball' with his friends and steal out at night to the Vaigai river, or the Pillaiyarpaliam tank, for a swim. He did not study Sanskrit, the *Vedas* or *Upanishads* (Hindu religious texts) in Madurai, as both the schools he attended were Christian, and he only learned about the Bible. As a youth, he was noted for his habit of sometimes falling into trance-like states. Once, one of his teachers told him to stand up on the bench for his failure to attend a lesson. Venkataraman gazed at him with such power and steadiness that his teacher's will withered away and the lad was excused.

One of his best school friends in Madurai was a Muslim boy nicknamed 'Sab Jan' whose real name was M. Abdul Wahab. Venkataraman said they were almost 'inseparable mates'. Later, Sab Jan recalled that, 'as a student Venkataraman was intensely religious', and most weekends they would visit Tiruparankunram and go around the beautiful Subramania Swami temple experiencing fervent ecstasy. Venkataraman would say, "God's creation is all alike and there is no difference in creation. God is the same, the apparent differences are created by man." Sab Jan said, "I then never felt any difference between a mosque and this temple." They also visited mother Azhagammal from time to time, where Sab Jan was equally well received.

It was in this house in Madurai, opposite the great temple of Meenakshi, that the young Venkataraman experienced his momentous spiritual awakening, which was to have such a great impact on world spirituality in time to come. It began in November 1895, when at the age of sixteen, he first heard the whereabouts of a holy mountain called Arunachala.

# Chapter Three

# THE MOMENT OF AWAKENING

*"I was born at holy Tiruchuzhi... in order that Shiva, the Absolute Consciousness, might shine forth and the Self flourish and I might be rescued from the misery of the world and the snares of the despicable senses, the Lord of the Red Hill raised me to his state."*

— V. 8, Arunachala Navamanimilai

Arunachala, the red mountain, on the Deccan Plain of Tamil Nadu, is not only geologically one of the oldest, but also one of the most revered mountains on the planet. It has been a sacred pilgrimage site for thousands of years. It is regarded as a monumental *linga* or symbol of Lord Shiva who once descended on this spot as a 'column of fire' to prove to Brahma and Vishnu that He was the most powerful among the gods. Over time, that column of fire transformed into a roseate-coloured mountain, in stark contrast to the smaller surrounding brownish hills.

One day, Venkataraman met an elderly relative and when he asked him where he was coming from, the answer was "from Arunachala!" He had known about this legendary place but now he knew that it was a mountain, and that it actually existed, and was located in Tiruvannamalai. At the same time, he found a copy of the scripture Periapuranam in his uncle's library. This famed biography of the notable sixty-three Tamil saints fired him to the depths. The young Venkataraman saw the beautifully carved statues of these saints in the temple of Meenakshi at Madurai, and waves of emotion overcame him. He prayed for Divine Grace to descend upon him, so that his devotion would become perpetual and that he, himself, would become like one of those Tamil saints.

Then in the middle of July 1896, in his uncle's house, he underwent that great transcendental experience which led to a profound spiritual awakening – that of Self-realisation and Enlightenment. He described this remarkable incident which changed his life irreversibly in the following words:

*A close-up of the main gopuram of the Meenakshi temple at Madurai.*

"It was about six weeks before I left Madurai for good that the great change in my life took place. It was so sudden! One day, I sat up alone on the first floor of my uncle's house. I was in my usual health. I seldom had any illness. I was a heavy sleeper, so on that day as I sat alone there was nothing wrong with my health. But a sudden and unmistakable fear of death seized me. I felt I was going to die. Why I should have so felt cannot now be explained by anything felt in my body. Nor could I explain it to myself then. I did not however trouble myself to discover if the fear was well-grounded. I felt 'I was going to die', and at once set about thinking what I should do. I did not care to consult doctors or elders or even friends. I felt I had to solve the problem myself – there and then.

"The shock of the fear of death made me at once introspective or introverted. I said to myself, mentally that is, without uttering the words – 'Now, death has come. What does it mean? What is it that is dying? This body dies.' I dramatised the scene of death. I extended my limbs and held them rigid as though *rigor mortis* had set in. I imitated a corpse to lend an air of reality to my further investigation. I held my breath and kept my mouth closed, pressing the lips tightly together so that no sound might escape. Let not the word "I" or any other word be uttered! 'Well then', I said to myself, 'this body is dead. It will be carried stiff to the burning ground and there burnt and reduced to ashes. But with the death of this body, am "I" dead? Is the body "I"? This body is silent and inert. But I feel the full force of my personality and even the sound "I" within myself – apart from the body. So "I" am a spirit, a thing transcending the body. The material body dies, but the spirit transcending it cannot be touched by death. I am, therefore, the deathless spirit.'

"All this was not a mere intellectual process, but flashed before me vividly as living truth, something which I perceived immediately, without any argument almost. "I" was something very real, the only real thing in that state, and all the conscious activity that was connected with my body was centred on that. The "I" or my 'Self' was holding the focus of attention by a powerful fascination from that time onwards. Fear of death had vanished once and forever.

"Absorption in the 'Self' has continued from that moment right up to this time. Other thoughts may come and go like the various notes of a musician, but the "I" continues like the basic or fundamental *sruti* note which accompanies and blends with all other notes. Whether the body was engaged in talking, reading or anything else, I was still centred on "I"."

Later, he said, "Previous to that crisis I had no clear perception of my 'Self', and was not consciously attracted towards it. I had felt no direct perceptible interest in it, much less any permanent disposition to dwell upon it when I lay down."

This deep experience and practise of Self-Enquiry took barely half-an-hour. The fear of death vanished and the real "I" engrossed all his attention, with marked reactions on his worldly life. He lost all interest in his studies, his relatives, and his companions as well. He developed the virtues of humility, gentleness and equanimity. He took his food without indulging in the carnal sensations of flavour and aroma.

The change was most marked in his approach to the great Meenakshi temple. Previously, if he went to the temple it was often with his friends, but now he went alone every day to contemplate Lord Shiva as Nataraja, Meenakshi and the Tamil saints. He later said that, "I would occasionally pray for the descent of grace upon me so that devotion might increase and become perpetual like that of the sixty-three saints. Mostly, I would not pray at all; but let the deep within flow on and on, into the deep without. Tears would mark this outflow of the soul but not betoken any particular feeling of pleasure or pain."

Nearly six weeks passed in this way. His relatives noticed the change but did not altogether approve, especially when they found him neglecting his studies. The crisis came on August 29, 1896. He had been set a task; to copy out a chapter from *Bain's Grammar* three times. He was writing the third copy, when there was a sudden repulsion. He bundled up his books and sat erect in meditation with his eyes closed. Then his elder brother Nagaswami, who was watching him all the while, strongly rebuked him. "Why should one who behaves thus retain all this?" Similar remarks had been constantly passed in the last few days, but had remained unnoticed. This time they drove home!

*The great bathing tank of the Meenakshi temple at Madurai.*

'Yes', thought Venkataraman, 'what real business have I here?' And, immediately, the thought of Arunachala arose. He got up and told his brother that he had to go to school to attend a special class, whereupon Nagaswami said, "Then do not fail to take five rupees from the box below and pay my college fees." With a pounding heart, he sped towards the Meenakshi temple, where all its gates and doors were auspiciously wide open and, remarkably, not another person was present. He then went to the innermost shrine to commune over his decision to leave home and live at Arunachala.

He understood that his family would be reluctant to let him go, so he decided to leave secretly. He took the five rupees his brother had set aside for college fees. He found a railway timetable and searched for the nearest station to Tiruvannamalai, and saw it was Tindivanam. He left a short note which said: "I have, in search of my father and in obedience to his command, started from here. This is only embarking on a virtuous enterprise. Therefore, none need grieve over this affair. To trace this (his travel route) out no money need be spent. Your college fee has not yet been paid. Two rupees are enclosed herewith."

His great, momentous adventure had now begun.

Chapter Four

# THE ROAD TO ARUNACHALA

*"Arunachala is the place, that which of all places deserves to
be called the holy place! Of all places it is the greatest! Know
that it is the Heart Centre of the Earth. It is Shiva Himself.
It is a secret place representing the Spiritual Heart. Lord Shiva
always abides there as a glorious hill called Arunachala!"*

– V. 1, Sri Arunachala Mahatmya

Venkataraman arrived at Madurai station and bought a
ticket to Tindivanam, preparing inwardly for his miraculous
journey. He did not know that there was now a new
station recently opened at Tiruvannamalai. The information
was given to him later by a co-passenger, a *maulvi* –
a Muslim religious scholar, who mysteriously was not
found in the compartment a short time later. He reached
Villupuram at three in the morning. He then went into the

21

town to ask the way to Arunachala. Feeling hungry, he ordered a meal but the innkeeper refused to accept any payment. With his remaining rupees, he bought a ticket to the next station and then decided he would walk to the holy mountain from there. A glorious, welcoming sunset saw him at Araiyaninallur where, in the temple there, he was visited by a vision of a brilliant, dazzling light.

The next day on Gokulashtami, the festival celebrating the birth of Lord Krishna, a pious couple gave him a substantial meal. He asked his host for a loan of four rupees on the pledge of his ruby and gold earrings. This request was accepted and he was able to take the train to Tiruvannamalai, reaching there around noon on September 1, 1896.

He went straight to the great Arunachaleswara temple. As he approached the doors, he found them open, but not a soul was present. He then went to the innermost shrine and paid his obeisance to Arunachala. Then after throwing the remainder of the money in a tank not far from the temple, he tore a strip from his cloth to make a loincloth. As he passed, an onlooker asked him if he wanted his head to be shaved. He agreed and off came his handsome locks. Then there was a sudden, short shower of rain which he regarded as a bath of grace. He re-entered the temple and proceeded with his absorption in the Self, at the thousand-pillared hall commonly known as a *Mandapam*.

His first night in Tiruvannamalai was spent freezing in the open-pillared hall in front of the temple. On the day of his arrival he had nothing to eat. Only the following day did he receive his first *bhiksha* or alms. He reported, "The next day I was walking up and down in the sixteen-pillared Mandapam in front of the temple, when a *Mauni* swami (one who observes the vow of silence), came there.

"Then another swami, named Palni, also came there. He was a well-built man with long, matted hair who used to do a great deal of service by clearing and cleansing the temple precincts with the help of a band of sannyasins. Then the Mauni swami, looking at me, a stranger in a hungry and exhausted condition, made signs to Palni swami that I should be given some food. Thereupon, Palni swami went and brought some cold rice, in a tin vessel which was all black, with a little salt strewn on top of the rice. That was the first bhiksha which Lord Arunachaleswara gave me!"

Venkataraman first settled down in the magnificent thousand-pillared hall in the temple compound, which is situated on the right when entering the temple through the eastern tower. Here, there is a constant coming and going of pilgrims. Exposed to the gaze of the general public in a place of pilgrimage, the strange youth soon aroused the curiosity of visitors. Street urchins started to pester and provoke him. No doubt they felt challenged by a youth the same age as themselves, sitting motionless like a statue in silent meditation. They would throw stones and potsherds at the boy and make fun of him. All this torment, the young Venkataraman withstood with motionless and silent forbearance.

Eventually, to escape their attention, he took refuge in an underground place, the Patala lingam, which few had the courage to face. Nobody knows the exact length of his stay there but when he was discovered, although still in *samadhi*, or a spiritual trance, blood and pus had oozed from his body, as the spot was favoured by rats. The intense *tapas* – severe spiritual discipline – of this young brahmin Swami, as he came to be called, was noticed by the temple attendants and the local sadhus. So eventually, he moved to the Mangai Pillayar temple where he met his first constant attendant, Uddandi Nayinar, who was keen to receive *upadesa*, or teaching, from him for Self-realisation.

The young, silent Swami started to attract attention there as well, and a number of pilgrims had begun to visit him. Venkataraman found their attentions irksome, so he moved to a suburb called Gurumurtam where he spent the next eighteen months, most of the time in samadhi. Here, the attendant arranged an *Abhishekam*, a sacred bath of water, milk, curd, etc., usually given to a deity, but just before the appointed time, he found these lines inscribed on the wall: "This food alone is the service needed for this body." These lines showed that the young Swami was literate, and a stubborn visitor refused to move until he revealed his identity. The Swami finally wrote, 'Venkataraman Tiruchuzhi'. This discovery soon became public and a report found its way to the ears of his relatives in Madurai.

In a few days, Nelliappier Iyer, Swami's uncle, was at Tiruvannamalai. Swami was then staying in a mango grove and visitors were strictly limited. But, when Nelliappier reached him, he was amazed to see his nephew, a dirt-laden Swami with matted hair and long nails, looking like an ancient rishi! He begged Swami to return home but his pleas elicited

*Shri Nelliappier Iyer*

*The young Venkataraman, seated on a slab of stone in the mango tree cave, when his uncle Nelliappier visited him at Tiruvannamalai.*

no response. Nelliappier returned to Madurai to report the news of his discovery to mother Azhagammal. She would not accept the fact that he refused to come home so, with Nagaswami, she went to Tiruvannamalai herself and found her son lying on a rock at Pavazhakunru. She made a determined effort, begging her boy to come home, with tears, appeals and upbraiding, but all was to no effect. Eventually, he replied by writing on a piece of paper these famous words:

'The ordainer controls the fate of souls in accordance with their *prarabdha karma* – their past deeds. Whatever is destined not to happen, will not happen. Whatever is destined to happen, will happen, do what you may to stop it. This is certain. The best course, therefore, is for one to be silent.'

Defeated, she returned to Madurai reluctantly leaving her son to live at Arunachala, moving from one cave to another as he so desired.

Before describing his early days on the hill, we must take note of how the young Swami had moved from his earlier phase of *bhakti* or devotion at Madurai, to Self-Enquiry – the means and direct consequence of his first death experience leading to Enlightenment.

Self-Enquiry was to eventually become the master key of his Teaching, later given to his devotees in their earnest quest for liberation. He brought this ancient practice, scattered in early classical Advaita texts such as the *Yoga Vasistha*, into a form suitable for the modern age, with many suggestions for its practise. Self-Enquiry had previously been reserved for the brahmin initiates of traditional gurus, but the young Swami was to make this sadhana an open secret for all who were drawn to the quest for Self-realisation, and release from the bondage of samsara, regardless of their background or nationality.

His move to Arunachala was replete with spiritual significance. As he himself wrote in his poem *Sri Arunachala Mahatmya*, quoting from the *Skanda Purana*:

"Arunachala is the place which deserves to be called the holy place! Of all places it is the greatest! Know that it is the Heart Centre of the Earth. It is Shiva Himself. It is a secret place representing the Spiritual Heart. Lord Shiva always abides there as a glorious hill called Arunachala... I, the Lord Shiva, ordain that those who reside within a radius of three *yojanas* (thirty miles) of this place shall attain union with the Supreme which removes bondage even in the absence of initiation."

*Seen in this picture are Venkataraman and his mother Azhagammal outside the Virupaksha cave when she came to visit him at Arunachala.*

Arunachala has been a sacred place of pilgrimage for thousands of years. Great sages, saints and sadhus have visited and stayed there in its caves over the passing centuries.

The Puranas tell us that there was once an unsettled dispute between Lord Vishnu and Lord Brahma as to who was the superior. They sought the help of Lord Shiva to judge who was really the greatest. Lord Shiva grew into a huge blazing light, stretching between earth and heaven, and asked them to find its root and its crown. Brahma, agreeing to reach the crown, took the form of a swan and flew. He flew to a great height but could not reach the peak. In his upward flight, he caught hold of a 'Pandava' flower (*Pandanus Odoratissimus*) falling from Shiva's crown and requested the flower to bear a false witness that he collected it from Shiva's crown. Knowing this, Lord Shiva cursed Brahma that he would never be worshipped in a temple, and banished the Pandava flower from his adornment.

Lord Vishnu then took the form of a boar and kept digging down to reach Shiva's feet, but failed; Shiva was really pleased with the humility of Vishnu and took him to His heart. Both gods then recognised Lord Shiva as the Supreme deity.

Arunachala stands today, as it has since time immemorial, as a great Shiva linga, a sacred mountain worshipped and revered as God Himself, radiating immense spiritual power and grace for all those fortunate to visit it, and bask in its powerful presence.

When living on the Hill, the Swami moved from one cave to another to enjoy the deepest meditation and frequently enter into the blessed state of samadhi for long periods. After living in the Mango cave, he moved to the Virupaksha cave which was much cooler in the hot summers of Tamil Nadu. It was while in the Virupaksha cave that the Swami was inspired to compose, as he walked round the Hill with devotees, his great poem *The Marital Garland of Letters* consisting of 108 verses – an archetypal, mystical hymn of great spiritual significance, full of devotional fervour, and portraying the prayers and pleadings that take place between the Divine Lover and the Beloved Divine. It was chanted by the sadhus, who had now attached themselves to him, whenever they went into the town to beg for food. It has since become the anthem of his devotees worldwide and is sung weekly, and on all auspicious occasions in his *ashram* – the place where a guru or sage dwells alone or along with his disciples – especially during the grand *Karthigai Deepam* festival, when a huge beacon is

*The awe-inspiring, holy mountain of Arunachala at Tiruvannamalai in Tamil Nadu*

lit on the top of the mountain, and over a million people from all parts of Southern India walk around the Hill, many chanting this hymn on the auspicious night of the new moon.

During this time spent absorbed in the Self, in the sacred caves of Arunachala, the Swami attracted many spiritual-minded persons who were fascinated by the powerful presence of the young boy. Among the first to visit him was Shri Gambhiram Seshier who asked a series of questions, to which the Swami, as was his custom then, answered by writing down the answers, so as not to disturb his state of silence. The result of this conversation was the celebrated treatise *Self-Enquiry* that set out all the details of this innovative practice that he brought afresh to the world.

At that time Sivaprakasam Pillai also asked a question. As a consequence, the Swami delivered his seminal treatise *Who Am I?* This again sets out the principles of his wonderful practice that he regarded as the infallible Direct Path to Self-realisation, if practised earnestly and with persistence. He wrote:

"By incessantly pursuing within yourself the enquiry 'Who Am I?' you will know your true Self and attain salvation."

The next person to seek the grace of the Swami was the celebrated poetic genius, Sanskrit scholar and great yogi, the Kavyakantha Ganapati Muni Sastri, who, with his disciples, was also meditating and performing tapas on the Hill. This meeting proved to be most auspicious. After the Muni confessed his failure to attain Realisation, in spite of all his spiritual struggles, the Swami bestowed on him his powerful gaze for about fifteen minutes and, then breaking his silence, said in Tamil:

"If one watches from when the notion of "I" springs, the mind is absorbed into that. That is tapas. When a mantra is repeated, if attention is directed to the source whence the mantra sound is produced, the mind is absorbed in that. That is tapas."

Ganapati Muni was overwhelmed by the young Swami's answers and his palpable presence. He then declared, "In future, this Brahmana Swami should, from now on, always be known as Sri Bhagavan Ramana Maharshi!" Later the Muni composed an incomparably beautiful poem himself, *The Forty Verses in Praise of Sri Bhagavan.*\*

---

\* I have versified this from a prose translation and placed it as an appendix in the book.

The Muni's relationship with the Maharshi was very close and remarkable. Ramana called him 'Nayana' and they were friends and companions, swimming in the tanks, climbing the Hill, and discussing the principles of Advaita Vedanta together.

One amazing incident demonstrates Ramana's love for Nayana. Bhagavan said: "One day I was lying down... suddenly I felt my body carried up higher and higher, till all objects disappeared, and all around me was one mass of white light. Then suddenly the body descended and objects began to appear. I said to myself: evidently this is how siddhas appear and disappear. The idea occurred to me that I was at Thiruvothiyur... I went into the Ganapati temple... Then I woke up and found myself back lying in Virupaksha cave."

This miraculous event happened in 1908, while the Kavyakantha was in the Thiruvothiyur temple. Engaged in tapas, he experienced some major difficulty and had wished for Bhagavan to come and give him guidance. Immediately, he saw Bhagavan entering the temple and he prostrated. The Maharshi placed his hand upon his head, whereupon he felt something like an electric shock which he regarded as *hastadiksha,* the spiritual initiation of a disciple by the guru through the touch of his hand.

Another devout *bhakta* or disciple of these days was Ramasami Aiyar. He reports that on his second visit he prostrated himself before the young Ramana and said, "Jesus, and other great souls, came into the world to redeem sinners. Is there any hope for me?" Came back the swift, emphatic reply in English, "There is hope. Yes, there is hope!"

Then there was a woman known as Echammal. She had lost her husband and two children one after the other. When she came to Bhagavan for solace, he was sitting in silence. She sat before him for an hour and that time completely changed her feelings. She felt that by the grace of the Maharshi, all her sorrows had completely vanished. She moved to Tiruvannamalai to be near him and spent all her money in his service, continuously bringing plenty of food for him and his bhaktas.

So, Sri Bhagavan Ramana Maharshi, as he was now called, settled down peacefully in the sacred caves of Arunachala as a renunciate with his first disciples whom he silently guided on his chosen path.

*Ramana Maharshi was now addressed as Sri Bhagavan by those who visited him in the caves on Arunachala, the holy mountain.*

Chapter Five

# EARLY DAYS AT ARUNACHALA

*"Annamalai! As soon as Thou didst claim me, my body and soul were Thine. Can I then lack anything? What else can I desire? I think only of Thee, not of merit and demerit, O my Life, do as Thou wilt my Beloved, grant me only ever increasing love for Thy blessed feet."*

– V. 7, Arunachala Navamanimalai

It was around this time that the first Westerner was drawn to the Maharshi. He was an Englishman by the name of F. H. Humphreys, who was then Assistant Superintendent of Police for the entire Arcot District. He had recently met Ganapati Muni, and being of a religious disposition himself, enquired if there were any Self-realised souls living on the Hill. The Muni immediately took him to see Sri Bhagavan. He asked the Maharshi how he could help the world.

Bhagavan replied: "Help yourself first, and you will help the world... You are in the world; you are the world. You are not different from the world. Nor is the world different from you."

The Master advised him to push on in his endeavour to reach the highest state through self-surrender. Later, Humphreys retired from the Police Force and entered a Roman Catholic monastery in England.

During this time, Bhagavan's mother continued to visit him. At one time, she became ill, and her son devotedly looked after her for three weeks in the Virupaksha cave until she recovered. In 1900, her eldest son died. Her brother-in-law also died soon afterwards. This was followed by the death of her daughter-in-law, the wife of her youngest son. She then decided she must join her second son, now named Sri Bhagavan Ramana Maharshi, in Arunachala in 1916.

The Maharshi then moved to larger premises at a small house named Skandasramam, built for him on the mountain, overlooking the great temple in Tiruvannamalai. She began to cook for him, and was then joined by her youngest son, now a widower. During the years she lived with Bhagavan, he carefully, by subtle ways, prepared her for the supreme consummation of Self-realisation which he undertook to bestow on her by touch, on her death-bed in 1922. I will describe this momentous event in more detail in another chapter, but suffice to say she was buried, not cremated as was customary, as she was now a *Jnani* – a Self-realised person. Later, the temple of Matrubhuteshwar – the Mother's temple – was built, and became the focus and starting point of what was eventually to grow into the ever-enlarging Ramanasramam, when the Maharshi moved down the Hill to live there. From that day on, the number of devotees steadily increased and his Teaching began to spread to the West.

*The original shrine built by Sri Ramana for his mother at his ashram.*

When the Maharshi first moved there, water was needed. Soon after his mother's internment, Bhagavan pointed to a place nearby where, within two or three feet of digging, a spring was found. Later, this was enlarged to contain a deep well which serves the ashram to this very day. We shall return to Ramanasramam in later chapters, but first we must go back to the historic visit of Sivaprakasam Pillai in 1902.

*The Matrubhuteshwar, also known as the Mother's temple, as it is today at the Ramanasramam.*

# Chapter Six

# SIVAPRAKASAM PILLAI AND 'WHO AM I?'

*"Look within, ever seeking the Self with the inner eye, then will it be found, thus didst Thou direct me, beloved Arunachala!"*

— V. 44, Arunachala Aksharamanamalai

In these early days on the Hill, the youthful sage was always immersed in Self-awareness and Supreme Bliss. Seeker after seeker started trickling in. The flow started with Sivaprakasam Pillai. This early devotee was a Philosophy graduate who had an enquiring mind. In 1902, he came to Sri Bhagavan with a prepared list of questions. Bhagavan's memorable answers to these questions have formed the seminal basic text of his message to all mature aspirants seeking Self-realisation. During his lifetime, when new visitors came to the ashram, this text was given to them to study so that they had some knowledge of his core

Teaching. As Sri Bhagavan was still observing *mouna* or silence, he wrote his answers on paper at that time. He had previously answered questions on Self-Enquiry to Gambhiram Seshier, an early devotee. These answers were later published as *Self-Enquiry*, a valuable treatise which explains the different approaches to his hallowed practice of Atma Vichara. However, as his historic seminal text *Who Am I?* is of such importance, I append it in full below.

*Who Am I? – (Nan Yar?)*

As all living beings desire to be always happy, without misery, there is observed supreme love for one's self. Happiness alone is the cause for love. In order to gain that happiness which is one's nature, and which is experienced in the state of deep sleep where there is no mind, one should know one's self. For that, the path of knowledge, the enquiry of the form, "Who am I?", is the principal means.

1. *Who am I?*

The gross body which is composed of the seven humours (*dhatus*), I am not; the five cognitive sense organs, viz. the senses of hearing, touch, sight, taste, and smell, which apprehend their respective objects, viz. sound, touch, colour, taste, and odour, I am not; the five cognitive sense-organs, viz. the organs of speech, locomotion, grasping, excretion, and procreation, which have as their respective functions speaking, moving, grasping, excreting, and enjoying, I am not; the five vital airs, *prana* (vital breath), etc., which perform respectively the five functions of in-breathing, etc., I am not; even the mind which thinks, I am not; the nescience too, which is endowed only with the residual impressions of objects, and in which there are no objects and no functionings, I am not.

2. *If I am none of these, then who am I?*
After negating all of the above-mentioned as 'not this', 'not this', that Awareness which alone remains – that I am.

3. *What is the nature of Awareness?*
The nature of Awareness is existence-consciousness-bliss.

4. *When will the realisation of the Self be gained?*
When the world which is what-is-seen has been removed, there will be realisation of the Self which is the seer.

5. *Will there not be realisation of the Self even while the world is there (taken as real)?*
There will not be.

*Sri Ramana relaxing on the wall of his ashram.*

6. *Why?*

The seer and the object seen are like the rope and the snake. Just as the knowledge of the rope, which is the substrate, will not arise unless the false knowledge of the illusory serpent goes, so the realisation of the Self, which is the substrate, will not be gained unless the belief that the world is real is removed.

7. *When will the world, which is the object seen, be removed?*

When the mind, which is the cause of all cognitions and of all actions, becomes quiescent, the world will disappear.

8. *What is the nature of the mind?*

What is called 'mind' is a wondrous power residing in the Self. It causes all thoughts to arise. Apart from thoughts, there is no such thing as mind. Therefore, thought is the nature of mind. Apart from thoughts, there is no independent entity called the world. In deep sleep there are no thoughts, and there is no world. In the states of waking and dream, there are thoughts, and there is a also a world. Just as the spider emits the thread (of the web) out of itself and again withdraws it into itself, likewise the mind projects the world out of itself and again resolves it into itself.

When the mind comes out of the Self, the world appears. Therefore, when the world appears (to be real), the Self does not appear; and when the Self appears (shines), the world does not appear. When one persistently enquires into the nature of the mind, the mind will end, leaving the Self (as the residue). What is referred to as the Self is the *Atman*. The mind always exists only in dependence on something gross; it cannot stay alone. It is the mind that is called the subtle body or the soul (*jiva*).

9. *What is the path of enquiry for understanding the nature of the mind?*

That which arises as "I" in this body is the mind. If one enquires as to where in the body the thought "I" rises first, one would discover that it rises in the heart. That is the place of the mind's origin. Even if one constantly thinks "I", "I", one will be led to that place. Of all the thoughts that arise in the mind, the "I" thought is the first. It is only after the rise of this that the other thoughts arise. It is after the appearance of the first personal pronoun that the second and third personal pronouns appear; without the first personal pronoun there will not be the second and third.

10. *How will the mind become quiescent?*

By the enquiry 'Who am I?' The thought 'Who am I?' will destroy all other thoughts, and like the stick used for stirring the burning pyre, it will itself in the end get destroyed. Then, there will arise Self-realisation.

11. *What is the means for constantly holding on to the thought 'Who am I?'*

When other thoughts arise, one should not pursue them, but should enquire: 'To whom do they arise?' It does not matter how many thoughts arise. As each thought arises, one should enquire with diligence, 'To whom has this thought arisen?' The answer that would emerge would be 'To me'. Thereupon if one enquires, 'Who am I?', the mind will go back to its source; and the thought that arose will become quiescent. With repeated practise in this manner, the mind will develop the skill to stay in its source.

When the mind, that is subtle, goes out through the brain and the sense organs, the gross names and forms appear; when it stays in the heart, the names and forms disappear. Not letting the mind go out, but retaining it in the heart is what is called *antar-mukha* or 'inwardness'. Letting the mind go out of the heart is known as *bahir-mukha* or 'externalisation'. Thus, when the mind stays in the heart, the "I" which is the source of all thoughts will go and the Self, whatever exists, will shine. Whatever one does, one should do without the egoity "I". If one acts in that way, all will appear as of the nature of Shiva (God).

12. *Are there no other means for making the mind quiescent?*

Other than enquiry, there are no adequate means. If through other means it is sought to control the mind, the mind will appear to be controlled but will again go forth. Through the control of breath also, the mind will become quiescent; but it will be quiescent only so long as the breath remains controlled and when the breath resumes, the mind also will again start moving and will wander as impelled by residual impressions. The source is the same for both mind and breath.

Thought, indeed, is the nature of the mind. The thought "I" is the first thought of the mind; and that is egoity. It is from that whence egoity originates that breath also originates. Therefore, when the mind becomes quiescent, the breath is controlled, and when the breath is controlled, the mind becomes quiescent. But in deep sleep, although the mind becomes quiescent, the breath does not stop. This is because of the will of God, so that the body may be preserved and other people may not be under the impression that it is dead. In the state of waking, and in samadhi, when the mind becomes quiescent the breath is controlled. Breath is the gross form of mind. Till the time of death, the mind keeps breath in the body; and when the body dies, the mind takes the breath along with it. Therefore, the exercise of breath-control is only an aid for rendering the mind quiescent (*manonigraha*); it will not destroy the mind (*manonasa*).

Like the practice of breath-control, meditation on the forms of God, repetition of mantras, restrictions on food, etc., are but aids for rendering the mind quiescent.

Through meditation on the forms of God and through repetition of mantras, the mind becomes one-pointed. The mind will always be wandering. Just as when a chain is given to an elephant to hold in its trunk, it will go along grasping the chain and nothing else, so also when the mind is occupied with a name or form, it will grasp that alone. When the mind expands in the form of countless thoughts, each thought becomes weak; but as thoughts get resolved, the mind becomes one-pointed and strong; for such a mind Self-Enquiry will become easy. Of all the restrictive rules, that relating to the taking of *sattvic* food, pure, light and vegetarian, in moderate quantities is the best; by observing this rule, the sattvic quality of mind will increase, and that will be helpful to Self-Enquiry.

13. *The residual impressions (thoughts) of objects appear to move like the waves of an ocean. When will all of them get destroyed?*

As the meditation on the Self rises higher and higher, the thoughts will get destroyed.

14. *Is it possible for the residual impressions of objects that come from beginningless time, as it were, to be resolved, and for one to remain as the pure Self?*

Without yielding to the doubt 'Is it possible, or not?', one should persistently hold on to the meditation on the Self. Even if one be a great sinner, one should not worry and weep, "Oh! I am a sinner, how can I be saved?"; one should completely renounce the thought "I am a sinner"; and concentrate keenly on meditation of the Self; then, one would surely succeed. There are not two minds – one good and the other evil; the mind is only one. It is the residual impressions that are of two kinds – auspicious and inauspicious. When the mind is under the influence of auspicious impressions, it is called good; when it is under the influence of inauspicious impressions, it is regarded as evil.

The mind should not be allowed to wander towards worldly objects and what concerns other people. However bad other people may be, one should bear no hatred for them. Both desire and hatred should be eschewed. All that one gives to others, one gives to one's self. If this truth is understood, who will not give to others? When one's self arises, all arises; when one's self becomes quiescent, all becomes quiescent. To the extent we behave with humility, to that extent there will result good. If the mind is rendered quiescent, one may live anywhere.

15. *How long should enquiry be practised?*

As long as there are impressions of objects in the mind, so long the enquiry "Who am I?" is required. As thoughts arise, they should be destroyed then and there in the very place of their origin, through enquiry. If one resorts to contemplation of the Self unintermittently, until the Self is gained, that alone would do. As long as there are enemies within the fortress, they will continue to sally forth; if they are destroyed as they emerge, the fortress will fall into our hands.

16. *What is the nature of the Self?*

What exists in truth is the Self alone. The world, the individual soul, and God are appearances in it. Like silver

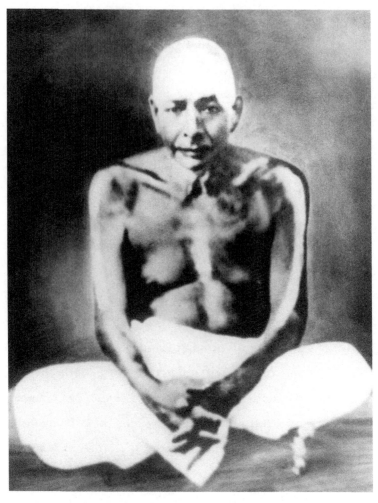

*Sri Sivaprakasam Pillai was one of the earliest devotees of Sri Ramana Maharshi.*

in mother-of-pearl, these three appear at the same time, and disappear at the same time. The Self is that where there is absolutely no "I" thought. That is called "Silence". The Self itself is the world; the Self itself is "I"; the Self itself is God; all is Shiva, the Self.

17. *Is not everything the work of God?*

Without desire, resolve, or effort, the sun rises; and in its mere presence, the sun-stone emits fire, the lotus blooms, water evaporates; people perform their various functions and then rest. Just as in the presence of the magnet the needle moves, it is by virtue of the mere presence of God that the souls governed by the three (cosmic) functions or the five-fold divine activity perform their actions and then rest, in accordance with their respective karmas. God has no resolve; no karma attaches itself to Him. That is like worldly actions not affecting the sun, or like the merits and demerits of the other four elements not affecting all-pervading space.

18. *Of the devotees, who is the greatest?*

He who gives himself up to the Self that is God is the most excellent devotee. Giving one's self up to God means remaining constantly in the Self without giving room for the rise of any thoughts other than that of the Self. Whatever burdens are thrown on God, He bears them.

Since the supreme power of God makes all things move, why should we, without submitting ourselves to it, constantly worry ourselves with thoughts as to what should be done and how, and what should not be done and how not? We know that the train carries all loads, so after getting on it why should we carry our small luggage on our head to our discomfort, instead of putting it down in the train and feeling at ease?

19. *What is non-attachment?*

As thoughts arise, destroying them utterly without any residue in the very place of their origin is non-attachment. Just as the pearl-diver ties a stone to his waist, sinks to the bottom of the sea and there takes the pearls, so each one of us should be endowed with non-attachment, dive within oneself and obtain the Self-Pearl.

20. *Is it not possible for God and the guru to effect the release of a soul?*

God and the guru will only show the way to release; they will not by themselves take the soul to the state of release. In truth, God and the guru are not different. Just as the prey which has fallen into the jaws of a tiger has no escape, so those who have come within the ambit of the guru's gracious look will be saved by him and will not get lost; yet, each one should by his own effort pursue the path shown by God or guru and gain release. One can know oneself only with one's own eye of knowledge, and not with somebody else's. Does he who is Rama require the help of a mirror to know that he is Rama?

21. *Is it necessary for one who longs for release to enquire into the nature of categories (tattvas)?*

Just as one who wants to throw away garbage has no need to analyse it and see what it is, so one who wants to know the Self has no need to count the number of categories or enquire into their characteristics; what he has to do is to reject altogether the categories that hide the Self. The world should be considered like a dream.

22. *Is there no difference between waking and dreaming?*

Waking is long and a dream short; other than this there is no difference. Just as waking happenings seem real while awake, so do those in a dream while dreaming. In dream, the mind takes on another body. In both waking and dream states – thoughts, names and forms occur simultaneously.

23. *Is there any use reading books for those who long for release?*

All the texts say that in order to gain release one should render the mind quiescent; therefore, their conclusive teaching is that the mind should be rendered quiescent; once this has been understood there is no need for endless reading. In order to quieten the mind one has only to enquire within oneself what one's Self is.

How could this search be done in books? One should know one's Self with one's own eye of wisdom. The Self is within the five sheaths; but books are outside them. Since the Self has to be enquired into by discarding the five sheaths, it is futile to search for it in books. There will come a time when one will have to forget all that one has learned.

24. *What is happiness?*

Happiness is the very nature of the Self; happiness and the Self are not different. There is no happiness in any object of the world. We imagine through our ignorance that we derive happiness from objects. When the mind goes out, it experiences misery. In truth, when its desires are fulfilled, it returns to its own place and enjoys the happiness that is the Self.

Similarly, in the states of sleep, samadhi and fainting, and when the object desired is obtained or the object disliked is removed, the mind becomes inward-turned, and enjoys pure Self-happiness. Thus the mind moves without rest, alternately going out of the Self and returning to it. Under the tree the shade is pleasant; out in the open the heat is scorching. A person who has been going about in the sun feels cool when he reaches the shade. Someone who keeps on going from the shade into the sun and then back into the shade is a fool. A wise man stays permanently in the shade. Similarly, the mind of the one who knows the truth does not leave *Brahman* – existence-consciousness-bliss. The mind of the ignorant, on the contrary, revolves in the world, feeling miserable, and for a little time returns to Brahman to experience happiness. In fact, what is called the world is only thought. When the world disappears, i.e. when there is no thought, the mind experiences happiness; and when the world appears, it goes through misery.

### 25. *What is wisdom-insight (jnana-drsti)?*

Remaining quiet is what is called wisdom-insight. To remain quiet is to resolve the mind in the Self. Telepathy, knowing past, present and future happenings, and clairvoyance do not constitute wisdom-insight.

*26. What is the relation between desirelessness and wisdom?*

Desirelessness is wisdom. The two are not different; they are the same. Desirelessness is refraining from turning the mind towards any object. Wisdom means the appearance of no object. In other words, not seeking what is other than the Self is detachment or desirelessness; not leaving the Self is wisdom.

*27. What is the difference between enquiry and meditation?*

Enquiry consists in retaining the mind in the Self. Meditation consists in thinking that one's self is Brahman.

*28. What is release?*

Enquiring into the nature of one's self that is in bondage, and realising one's true nature is release.

Sri Bhagavan's activities at the newly founded ashram began well before daybreak. He required hardly any sleep and rose early at 4 am. With other close devotees, they would then gather in what is now known as the old Hall for silent meditation and the chanting of *bhajans* or devotional songs. At dawn, they would enter the kitchen and he would lead them as a team to cut the vegetables

*Sri Ramana during his days in Skandasramam.*

and prepare the food for cooking – with full attention, quickly and with remarkable accuracy. He strictly demanded total equality in the sharing of food for all devotees alike. They would then retire for a light breakfast in the new, well-designed dining hall. Afterwards, the Maharshi would usually be engaged in literary work, correcting proofs or indicating replies to questions of correspondents though he never wrote letters himself. The other devotees went about their tasks such as gardening, *puja* (worship), cooking, or carrying out various odd jobs as they were needed. Lunch was served at 11:30 am, after the cows and the poor had been fed. Following the meal, the Maharshi would attend to any work which needed close attention such as book binding or leaf stitching. It was after three o'clock that visitors would come and questions would be addressed to the Maharshi reclining on his couch in the old Hall.

He answered sincere questions readily, and often gave his *darshan* – a ritual appearance before devotees, by an intensive gaze, teaching by Silence, like the primordial sage Dakshinamurti did, and evoking a glimpse of the real Self in the fortunate recipient. Fortunately, for all future generations, his answers to questions from 1935-39 were translated into English, which he himself approved, and later published in book form. These talks with Sri Ramana Maharshi are sheer gold and a constant source of inspiration to his devotees worldwide.

Sunset was regarded as the best time for meditation followed by a light supper and early nights. So, from a small seed that the ashram was planted, it flourishes today as a beautiful tree, efficiently run and managed by devoted members of his brother's family.

During these years, the Maharshi composed highly important texts, always in poetic form. These included more hymns to Arunachala, *The Essence of Instruction* or *Upadesa Saram*, the celebrated *Forty Verses on Reality* or *Ulladu Narpadu*, with a Supplement. He made, and improved, translations of important works of Adi Shankara from Sanskrit into Tamil, such as *The Crest Jewel of Discrimination* and the *Atma Bodha*. Sri Bhagavan's own Teachings are

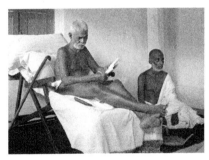

often equated with those of that great sage. We will now recount his important middle years at Arunachala which were full of great significance in every respect.

*Sri Ramana editing a manuscript.*

*This picture is known as the 'Dakshinamurti', as Bhagavan is seated facing the south.*

# Chapter Seven

# THE MIDDLE YEARS
# AT ARUNACHALA

*"Bearing and tending me in the world in the form of my father and mother, Thou didst enter my heart and before I fell into the deep sea of Universal Illusion and was drowned, Thou didst draw me to Thee and keep me at Thy Feet. How shall I describe Thy wonderful Grace, O Arunachala who art Consciousness Itself?"*

– V. 9, The Necklet of Nine Gems

There is no question that in his destiny as a *Jagadguru* or World Teacher, Sri Bhagavan Ramana Maharshi meant his Teaching to be available to the whole world. This was a great innovation as, previously, the supreme knowledge was secretive and reserved only for the Hindu brahmin initiates of traditional gurus.

Paul Brunton (Raphael Hurst) was a successful journalist from London who was interested in mysticism and comparative religion. He eventually travelled to India in

search of the real spiritual Truth, and for guidance he contacted the famed Kanchipitam Sankaracharya, who directed him to go and see Ramana Maharshi; as in the Sankaracharya's view, the Maharshi was the guru marked out for him by destiny. Brunton then had

*Paul Brunton, the journalist.*

several highly significant meetings and dialogues with Sri Bhagavan and was highly impressed. So much so, that his eventual book *A Search In Secret India*, where he records his travels and meetings with Sri Bhagavan, became an international best-seller throughout the United States of America and Europe, during the 1930s.

This led to many important Westerners visiting Arunachala to receive Sri Bhagavan's darshan, including Major Alan Chadwick O.B.E., later to remain and become Sadhu Arunachala, and the senior diplomat in Madras, Grant Duff. The noted Oxford scholar, Arthur Osborne, also arrived amongst many other learned devotees. The renowned international psychiatrist, C. G. Jung, wrote an eleven-page appreciation of the Maharshi in his introduction to Heinrich Zimmer's book *Der Weg zum Selbst* (The Way to the Self), which was later published in his *Collected Works*.

The Maharshi's special appeal to Westerners was founded not only on his serene presence, the palpable feeling of love and profound silence which emanated from him, but also by his simple Direct Teaching which made it possible to practise his recommended Self-Enquiry and Devotion, without having to change lifestyles, or necessarily take part in Hindu ceremonial practices.

We must now turn to the significant event surrounding Bhagavan's mother Azhagammal's demise, her liberation and her samadhi.

Mother Azhagammal was always particular that she should die in the arms of her beloved rishi son. She used to say, "Even if you were to throw away my dead body in these thorny bushes, I do not mind but I must end my life in your arms!" But to Bhagavan who saw everything exactly as it truly is, death was only a name, a mere matter of form. He said:

"What is death but a change of form, which calls for a fresh name? But as for the substance, that does not change."

In May 1922, his mother contracted a serious illness. All possible medical attention was lovingly bestowed upon her. Sri Ramana was often at her bedside, but her end seemed to be approaching. Bhagavan knew that his only remaining duty was to soothe her, and give her all the spiritual aid he could possibly muster at the point of her death. He placed his right hand on her heaving chest, and his left hand firmly on her head. This somehow symbolised the need for her mind to fall into the Spiritual Heart, an essential part of his great Teaching.

The devotees chanted *Rama Nama*, the name of Lord Rama, so she would be conscious of Brahman at her moment of death – as the *Gita* suggests. A struggle seemed to ensue between Sri Ramana and his mother. She evidently passed through a series of subtle experiences, but Bhagavan's touch generated a current which turned her soul back from its wandering into her heart. When all the *vasanas* or desires were destroyed, the soul was led into the heart of eternal peace and liberation, which was signified by a peculiar vibration of sound. Bhagavan commented:

"Here, the accumulated vasanas of the past rose up again and again, and then they were destroyed... I saw that the mother's prana was completely merged in the heart... it is over."

She left her body peacefully on the 19th of May. A samadhi was prepared and she was laid to rest. Nayana commented that her face shone brilliantly bright, glowing with a divine resplendence. She looked like a Self-realised yogini in deep meditation. Bhagavan was satisfied that through her sadhana and Divine Grace, she was now liberated.

As tradition demands in the case of a liberated being, the body was not cremated but buried at the foot of the Hill and a linga installed. Soon after, Bhagavan decided to move down from the Hill and live near his mother's samadhi. This led to the eventual building of a beautiful temple dedicated to the mother, which now gives aid and spiritual help to all devotees who pray and meditate at this sacred place.

*A child leads Sri Ramana up the steps towards the dining hall.*

# Chapter Eight

# SRI RAMANA'S LOVE FOR ANIMALS AND CHILDREN

*"He who dedicates his mind to Thee, and seeing Thee, always beholds the universe as Thy figure, he who at all times glorifies Thee and loves Thee as none other than the Self, he is the master without rival, being One with Thee. And lost in Thy Bliss, O Arunachala!"*

– V. 5, Arunachala Pancharatna

Earlier, I had mentioned that Sri Ramana could easily communicate with the birds and beasts of the animal kingdom.

Cows, squirrels, monkeys, cats, dogs and birds inhabiting the ashram were treated by him with the same loving care and equality as human beings. He would never allow any animal to be treated harshly. He is recorded as saying,

"We do not know what souls may be tenanting these bodies and for finishing what portion of their unfinished karma, they seek our company."

Famous among these animals was the cow named Lakshmi. She was said to be an incarnation of the 'Old Lady of the Greens' who fed Ramana at the turn of the century, who would meticulously walk around gathering green vegetables to cook for him and other devotees.

Lakshmi, the holy cow of the ashram.

The story of Lakshmi is remarkable and uniquely miraculous. She was housed in the *goshala* or cowshed, where she was the accepted leader of the immaculate herd of ashram cows. She always moved with the greatest dignity and often visited the main Hall where Bhagavan was reclining. When the inmates and attendants of the ashram would try to shoo her out, the Maharshi would always intervene saying, "Let her stay. She has come to invite me to her palace," referring to the goshala. At the appropriate time she would lead him there. She found an opportunity to meet Sri Bhagavan almost every day. He would talk to her, and she would nod in understanding.

Lakshmi passed away on June 18, 1948. A little earlier, the Maharshi sitting on the hay by her side, lifted her head with both his hands, and passing one of his hands lightly over her face and throat, and then placing his left hand on the head began pressing her throat, right down to her heart, with the fingers of his right hand. With his divine touch, the outer breath of Lakshmi and the movement of the body began to decrease. She experienced no agony of death because Bhagavan had helped her in attaining *moksha* (salvation).

Sri Ramana had often mentioned that some animals who were reincarnated human beings, could be liberated at death. A samadhi was built for Lakshmi opposite Sri Bhagavan's Hall. Pujas in her memory are still regularly held at her tomb. Her epitaph, composed by Bhagavan himself, in Tamil, reads: "It is hereby recorded that Lakshmi the cow was liberated under the star of Visakha, on Friday the twelfth day of the bright half of Jyeshta, in the year Sarvadhari."

There were many dogs in the ashram then, as there are today. One dog, named Chinna Karuppan, was described by Bhagavan as "A person of high principles. When we were in the Virupaksha cave, something black used to pass, but at a distance. We would be able to see his head peeping over the bushes sometimes. His *vairagya*, non-attachment, appeared to be very strong. He kept company with none, in fact he seemed to avoid company. We respected his independence and vairagya and used to leave food near his place and go away. One day, as we were going up the Hill, Kuruppan suddenly jumped across the path and romped upon me, wagging his tail in glee …thereafter, he was with us in the ashram as one of the inmates."

Kamala was another remarkable dog. "Take this stranger around," Sri Ramana would say, and she would take the person to every cave, tank, and around the Hill. Another dog named Jackie was a great *tapasvi* – an ascetic. He would eat only what was offered to him and spent the rest of his time in a kennel-like cave near the Maharshi, sitting in silence and peace. Jackie was given the honour of being buried in the ashram precincts, with a little tomb raised over the spot.

Whenever the monkeys in the ashram had a dispute, they would consult the Maharshi who would advise and resolve their problems, and send them away satisfied. In one such case, there was unrest among the followers of the

*Sri Ramana taking a walk near the ashram with one of his favourite dogs.*

Monkey King, who had ostracised two group members. Suddenly, the King left on the Maharshi's advice and, after two weeks of tapasya in the forest, returned and challenged his critics, who then gave up the quarrel. There was no further trouble. There are many stories which have been published by Ramanasramam that tell of the numerous interactions between Bhagavan and other animals, including leopards, during his lifetime. Even the serpents were often companions in his caves.

He once settled a war among the squirrels and they would often affectionately run all over his couch, scurry into its sides and under the pillows. He also paid special attention to a deer named Valli by attending to her wounded leg. On her last day on earth, Bhagavan put her head on his thigh and went on patting her. After midnight, Bhagavan returned to his couch. Valli had attained *mukti* – salvation, at the hands of the Lord of Compassion! Valli was also buried in the ashram and there is a tomb for her as well. He also fondly cared for a lame cat that had once strayed from the ashram, and took special interest in the affairs of the peacocks who resided there.

Once, as he was passing along a forest on the Hill, his left thigh accidentally rubbed against a hornet's nest and disturbed the hive. Before he could move away, the hornets came buzzing, settled on the same thigh and stung his flesh. "Yes, yes, that is the leg that disturbed your nest. Let it suffer," he said. He refused to move until the hornets were satisfied with the punishment, and then they flew away.

These stories are indeed remarkable and illustrate his greatness as a Supreme Guru, and show us that an evolved human being can be truly loved by the animal kingdom. In a sense, it presages the biblical prophecy that in the Messianic Age, there will be an evolved humanity, when the lamb shall lie down with the lion, and conditions shall return to what they were in the Garden of Eden.

Sri Bhagavan showed a great interest, kindness and consideration with many of the children of the devotees who lived in the ashram. There are many enchanting incidents recorded by Kitty, daughter of the distinguished Oxford professor and author Arthur Osborne, an ashram resident, who wrote many important books on Bhagavan's Teachings. Once Bhagavan said to her, "If Kitty thinks of me, I shall think of her." This remark stayed with her and formed the auspicious background to her childhood and life ever since.

*Sri Ramana (seated above) with the children of his devotees in the ashram.*

One day, his devotees C. Somasundaram and Uma Pillai brought their six-year-old son Natarajan to Bhagavan. When they entered the ashram, the boy remarked, "I have been here before!" He recalled many memories of his life in the ashram. Sri Bhagavan then took a great interest in the boy because he had probably been an ashramite in a previous birth.

Janaki Mata from Tanjore was one of Bhagavan's great devotees. Her daughter Padma Sitapati had a son Janakiramanan who had lost his eyesight when he was only three years old. Padma wrote a letter to Bhagavan in which she appealed for his Grace. The reply came back, "By the Grace of Bhagavan, the child Janakiramanan's eyesight will be fully restored." For forty days, the boy could not open his eyes. On Karthigai Deepam day, the boy was taken to the Tanjore temple. Suddenly, he began to see images. He was brought home, and started seeing well. He shouted "I am seeing Bhagavan, I am seeing Mataji!" But the child still suffered from night blindness, Padma told Bhagavan. He looked steadily at the boy, who was then able to see Bhagavan's head. The boy's night blindness had gone.

V. Ganesan, the former Editor of the *Mountain Path*, says, "When I was three or four years old, a memorable incident occurred. I was a very healthy, plump and chubby child. I was the favourite of the elderly women who worked as kitchen assistants. They pampered me and I was fascinated with the serving of food, and how Bhagavan used to nod his head as a sign that everyone could eat, now that everyone had been served. He was very strict on equality amongst all.

"One day I felt an urge to serve food to Bhagavan and the others. I was very short and the assistants refused to give me permission. I cried and created a hubbub. Sri Bhagavan noticed the commotion and after enquiring what it was all about, told the kitchen assistant, "Give him a very small cup of salt and a tiny spoon. Let him put a little salt on each leaf." All my crying stopped and I completed my task quickly after Sri Bhagavan told me how much salt to put. While returning from the Hill, he once pinched my hand noticing that my name was written there. He said, "I have pinched Ganesan and not 'you'. What is Ganesan? Is it the hand?"

There are many such stories that illustrate his affectionate care and love of small children. Surely his ability to converse with the animal kingdom, and to 'suffer little children', contribute to demonstrate his greatness and add to his undoubted reputation as a Supreme Guru.

*Sri Ramana sitting in sukhasana with Chinnaswami and Daivarata.*

Chapter Nine

# GREAT SAGES COME TO MEET
# SRI RAMANA

*"I, by Thy Grace am sunk in Thy Self, wherein merge
only those divested of their minds and thus made pure,
O Arunachala!"*

– V. 47(b), Sri Arunachala Mahatmya

Several devotees attained the glorious, exalted state of
Self-realisation through Bhagavan's instruction and grace.
His grandnephew, V. Ganesan, who was living in the
ashram from his childhood to manhood, once told me
that in his estimation at least forty devotees attained
moksha during his lifetime. Not all came to be known
as Jnanis who taught from their own ashrams. Most of
them preferred to live a life as householders, spreading
their influence quietly and silently, but some did become
well known sages, after Bhagavan's *Mahasamadhi* – conscious
casting off of the mortal body.

*Swami Ramdas*

One of these was the famed Swami Ramdas, founder of the Anandashram at Kanhangad. Here is a beautiful story, as related in the *Mountain Path*. In his early autobiography *In Quest of God* (published by Anandashram, Kanhangad), Swami Ramdas describes how he attained the Divine Vision through the Grace of the Maharshi. Years later, he told this story to Dilip Kumar Roy who reproduced it in his book *The Flute Calls Still:*

"'Papa', I said, 'would you mind telling us about your final Realisation which they call *Vishvarupa darshan?*' He readily acquiesced and gave a long description of the burning aspiration and yearning which had led him to Arunachala Hill, hallowed by the tapas of the famous sage Sri Ramana Maharshi.

"One day the kind Sadhuram took Ramdas for the darshan of Sri Ramana Maharshi. His ashram was at the foot of Arunachala. Both visitors entered the ashram and, meeting the sage, I prostrated at his holy feet. He was young but there was on his face a calmness, and in his large eyes a passionless look of tenderness which cast a spell of peace and joy on all those who came to him. Ramdas was informed that the sage knew English, so he addressed him thus: 'Maharaj, here stands before thee a humble slave. Have pity on him. His only prayer to thee is to give him thy blessing.'

"The Maharshi turned his beautiful eyes towards Ramdas and looked intently for a few minutes into his eyes, as though he was pouring into Ramdas his blessing through those orbs, then shook his head to say he had blessed. A thrill of inexpressible joy coursed through Ramdas, his whole body quivering like a leaf in the breeze ... Now at the prompting of Ram, Ramdas desired to remain in solitude for some time ... Sadhuram was ever ready to fulfil his wishes.

"Losing no time, he took Ramdas up to the mountain behind the great temple. Climbing high up, he showed him many caves. Of these, one small cave was selected for Ramdas which he occupied the next day. In this cave, he lived for nearly a month in deep meditation of Lord Rama. This was the first time he was taken by Ram into solitude for his bhajan. Now he felt most blissful sensations since he could hold undisturbed communion with Rama.

He was actually rolling in a sea of indescribable happiness. To fix the mind on that fountain of bliss, Rama, means to experience pure joy ... He went on taking the name in an ecstasy of longing when, lo, suddenly his Lord Rama ... appeared before him and danced and danced.

"'Did you see him with closed eyes or open?' I interjected. 'With open eyes, as Ramdas is seeing you,' Papa answered. But it was not this momentary vision that Ramdas's heart craved. For he knew that a vision like this was unlikely to last and so, when the Lord would vanish, Ramdas would revert to his darkness. Therefore, he prayed for the great darshan, the Vision of visions, which comes to stay forever so there is no more parting – namely the *Vishvarupa darshan*, the longing to see Rama always in everything; nothing less would satisfy Ramdas.

"Papa paused and then resumed with a beatific smile: 'And it came one morning apocalyptically – when, lo, the entire landscape changed. All was Rama, nothing but Rama – wherever Ramdas looked! Everything was ensouled by Rama – vivid, marvellous, rapturous – the trees, the shrubs, the ants, the cows, the cats, the dogs – even inanimate things pulsated with the marvellous presence of the one Rama. And Ramdas danced in joy, like a boy who, when given a lovely present, can't help breaking out into a dance.'

"And so it was with Ramdas. He danced with joy and rushed at a tree which he embraced, because it was not a tree but Rama Himself! A man was passing by and Ramdas ran towards him and embraced him, calling out: 'Rama, O Rama!' The man got scared and bolted. But Ramdas gave him chase and dragged him back to his cave. The man noted that Ramdas had not a tooth in his head and so felt a little reassured: at least the loony would not be able to bite him! He laughed out and we swelled the chorus. 'And then?' I asked, after the laughter had subsided. 'The bliss and joy came to be permanent, like a torrent rushing downhill till it finds a placid level of limpid purling stream. This experience is called *Sahaja Samadhi*, in which you can never be cut off from the consciousness of being at one with the One who has become all, in which you feel you are one with all because you have perceived that all is He, the One-without-a-second.'"

Finally we end with a comment made, about forty years later, by Swami Ramdas in *Vision*, the monthly journal published by Anandashram, "Ramdas went to

Ramana Maharshi in a state of complete obliviousness of the world. He felt thrills of ecstasy in his presence. The Maharshi made the awakening permanent in Ramdas."

*Sri Hariwansh Lal Poonja*

The next sage to receive Self-realisation from Sri Bhagavan was the highly influential and renowned Hariwansh Lal Poonja, better known to the world as Papaji. In his excellent three-volume biography of Papaji entitled *Nothing Ever Happened,* the author David Godman tell us how Papaji met Sri Bhagavan at Tiruvannamalai.

"A sadhu came to my door, asking for food. I invited him in, offered him some food and asked him the question that was uppermost in my mind. 'Can you show me God? If not, do you know of anyone who can?' Much to my surprise he gave me a positive answer. 'Yes, I know a person who can show you God. If you go and see that man, everything will be all right for you. His name is Ramana Maharshi.'

"I followed the sadhu's advice and travelled by train to

Tiruvannamalai. On alighting there, I discovered that the Maharshi's ashram was about three kilometres away on the other side of the town. So, I engaged a bullock cart to take me and my belongings there. As soon as we reached the ashram, I jumped out of the cart, put my bags in the men's dormitory, and went off to look for this man who could show me God. I peeped in through his window and saw, sitting on a sofa inside, the same man who had visited my house in the Punjab... Sri Ramana Maharshi! I approached him in a belligerent manner. 'Are you the man who came to see me at my house in the Punjab?' I demanded. The Maharshi remained silent. I tried again. 'Did you come to my house and tell me to come here? Are you the man who sent me here?' Again the Maharshi made no comment. Since he was unwilling to answer either of these questions, I moved on to the main purpose of my visit. 'Have you seen God?' I asked, 'And if you have, can you enable me to see him? I am willing to pay any price, even my life, but your part of the bargain is that you must show me God.'

"'No', he answered, 'I cannot show you God or enable you to see God because God is not an object that can be seen. God is the subject. He is the seer. Don't concern yourself with objects that can be seen. Find out who the seer is.' He also added, 'You alone are God', as if to rebuke

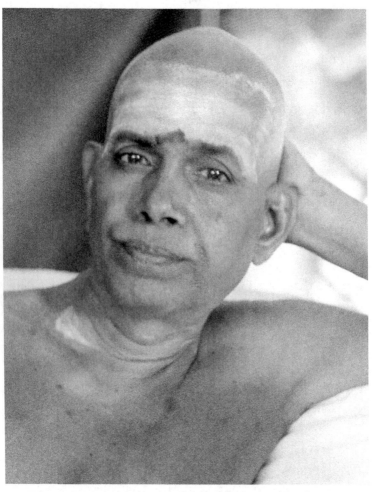

*Sri Ramana's gaze penetrated deep into the hearts of his devotees.*

me for looking for a God who was outside and apart from me. At the conclusion of his words he looked at me and, as he gazed into my eyes, my whole body began to tremble and shake. A thrill of nervous energy shot through my body. My nerve endings felt as if they were dancing and my hair stood on end. Within me, I became aware of the Spiritual Heart. This is not the physical heart. It is, rather, the source and support of all that exists. Within this Heart, I saw or felt something like a closed bud. It was very shiny and bluish. With the Maharshi looking at me, and with myself in a state of inner silence, I felt this bud open and bloom. I use the word 'bud' but this is not an exact description. It would be more correct to say that something that felt bud-like opened and bloomed within me in the Heart. And when I say 'Heart', I don't mean that the flowering was located in a particular place in the body. This Heart, this Heart of my Heart, was neither inside the body nor out of it. I can't give a more exact description of what happened.

"All I can say is that in the Maharshi's presence, and under his gaze, the Heart opened and bloomed. It was an extraordinary experience, one that I had never had before. I had not come looking for any kind of experience, so it totally surprised me when it happened.

"I stayed there for about a week, immersed in my devotional practices. Krishna would often appear before me, and we spent a lot of time playing together."

*Sri Ramana Maharshi sitting in the porch at Skandasramam.*

Chapter Ten

# LATER YEARS AT ARUNACHALA

*"I have discovered a new thing! This hill, the lodestone of lives,
arrests the movements of anyone who so much as thinks of it,
draws him face to face with it, and fixes him motionless like
itself, to feed upon his soul thus ripened. What a wonder is
this! Oh Souls! Beware of It and live! Such a destroyer of lives
is this magnificent Arunachala, which shines within the Heart!"*

— V. 10, Eleven Verses to Arunachala

There is a reasonably good road around Arunachala,
and Sri Bhagavan recommended that his devotees should
practice *Giripradakshina* (take a slow walk around the Hill),
like a pregnant woman, with reverence and attention. This
practice would be of spiritual and physical benefit as the
natural herbs growing in the vicinity filled the air with a
healing fragrance. Sri Bhagavan himself often took this walk

*Devotees performing the Giripradakshina of Arunachala – the holy mountain.*

of around fourteen kilometres himself, until age caught up with him and his body became too frail to continue. Today, on the Karthigai Deepam festival, when a beacon is set alight on top of Arunachala, at full moon, over a million people walk on this route, many chanting his famous hymn, *The Marital Garden of Letters,* as they proceed.

During his later years, many important visitors from the West came to receive his darshan, as well as Indians of all castes and religious persuasions.

Among the illustrious Western visitors who came to

receive Sri Bhagavan's darshan was the author Paul Brunton. Here is the report published in Ramanasramam's famous spiritual journal the *Mountain Path* describing Brunton's initial meeting with the Maharshi.

It was half-past four in the afternoon, and the disciples were sitting before the Maharshi in the hall and talking about a notification that had appeared in the newspapers to the effect that a Mr. Paul Brunton was planning to visit the ashram. The clock struck five and there entered a man in European dress, bearing a plate of sweets. The visitor offered the sweets to the Maharshi and then, after making obeisance in the Eastern way, he squatted on the floor before him.

The man was Paul Brunton, a London journalist who was then on a visit to India. He was keenly interested in the spiritual teaching of the East and thought that, by an intelligent study and appreciation of it, the cause of cooperation between East and West might be greatly promoted. He came to Sri Ramanasramam after visiting many other ashrams. He sat spellbound before Maharshi and there was pin-drop silence. The silence was broken by the person who had brought the visitor, asking him if he would like to ask any questions.

He was, however, not in a mood to do so and thus an hour-and-a-half passed. Brunton then stated the purpose of his visit. In a voice of intense earnestness, he said that he had come to India for spiritual enlightenment. "Not only myself," he added, "but many others also in the West are longing for the Light from the East."

The Maharshi sat completely indrawn and paid no attention. Early next morning, the visitor entered the hall and put some questions to the Maharshi with great earnestness. The conversation reproduced below is from rough notes taken while it was going on:

*Brunton: Many people do meditate in the West but show no signs of progress.*

Maharshi: How do you know that they don't make progress? Spiritual progress is not easily discernible.

*Brunton: A few years ago I got some glimpses of bliss but in the years that followed I lost it again. Then last year I again got it. Why is that?*

Maharshi: You lost it because your meditation had not become natural (*sahaja*). When you become habitually in-turned, the enjoyment of spiritual beatitude becomes a normal experience.

*Brunton: Might it be due to the lack of a guru?*

Maharshi: Yes, but the guru is within; that guru who is within is identical with your Self.

*Brunton: What is the way to God-realisation?*

Maharshi: Vichara; asking yourself the question 'Who am I?' – an enquiry into the nature of your Self.

*Brunton: Does the Maharshi know whether an avatar already exists in the physical body?*

Maharshi: He might.

*Brunton: What is the best way to attain Godhood?*

Maharshi: Self-Enquiry leads to Self-realisation.

*Brunton: Is a guru necessary for spiritual progress?*

Maharshi: Yes.

*Brunton: Is it possible for the guru to help the disciple forward on the path?*

Maharshi: Yes.

*Brunton: What are the conditions for discipleship?*

Maharshi: Intense desire for Self-realisation, earnestness and purity of mind.

*Brunton: Is it necessary to surrender one's life to the guru?*

Maharshi: Yes. One should surrender everything to the Dispeller of Darkness. One should surrender the ego that binds one to this world. Giving up body-consciousness is the true surrender.

*Brunton: Does a guru want to take control of the disciple's worldly affairs also?*

Maharshi: Yes, everything.

*Brunton: Can he give the disciple the spiritual spark that he needs?*

Maharshi: He can give him all that he needs. This can be seen from experience.

*Brunton: Is it necessary to be in physical contact with the guru and, if so, for how long?*

Maharshi: It depends on the maturity of the disciple. Gunpowder catches fire in an instant, while it takes time to ignite coal.

*Brunton: Is it possible to develop along the path of the Spirit while leading a life of work?*

Maharshi: There is no conflict between work and wisdom. On the contrary, selfless work paves the way to Self-knowledge.

*Brunton: If a person is engaged in work it will leave him little time for meditation.*

Maharshi: It is only spiritual novices who need to set aside a special time for meditation. A more advanced person always enjoys the beatitude whether he is engaged in work or not. While his hands are in society, he can keep his head cool in solitude.

There were many subsequent meetings, and Brunton visited his new-found guru many times. He recorded many of his dialogues in his book, *A Search in Secret India* and later, from his notebooks, Ramanasramam published *Conscious Immortality,* a further record of his discussions with the Maharshi.

*Ramana Maharshi flanked by Paul Brunton (right) and a devotee.*

Another important visitor was the well-known English novelist, Somerset Maugham, a friend of Paul Brunton. Here are extracts from an article in the *Mountain Path* describing his visit.

*William Somerset Maugham, popular English novelist and playwright (1874-1965).*

In January 1938, Somerset Maugham, the British novelist, visited Ramanasramam for a few hours. The brief contact he had with Bhagavan inspired Maugham so much, he decided to use him as the model for a fictional guru in *The Razor's Edge,* his masterpiece which was published a few years later in 1944. Maugham also wrote a non-fiction account of his visit in an essay entitled *The Saint,* which was published twenty years after the event in 1958. The following account, which is taken from this essay, records Maugham's impressions of this meeting with Bhagavan.

"He uttered a few words of cordial greeting and sat on the ground not far from the pallet on which I lay.

"After the first few minutes during which his eyes with a gentle benignity rested on my face, he ceased to look at me but, with a sidelong stare of peculiar fixity, gazed as it were, over my shoulder. His body was absolutely still, but now and then one of his feet tapped lightly on the earthen floor. He remained thus, motionless, for perhaps fifteen minutes; and they told me later that he was concentrating in meditation upon me. Then he came to, if I may so put it, and again looked at me. He asked me if I wished to say anything to him, or ask any question. I was feeling weak and ill and said so; whereupon he smiled and said, 'Silence is also conversation.' He turned his head away slightly and resumed his concentrated meditation, again looking, as it were, over my shoulder. No one said a word; the other persons in the hut, standing by the door, kept their eyes riveted upon him. After another fifteen minutes, he got up, bowed, smiled farewell and, slowly leaning on his stick, he limped out of the hut followed by his disciples.

Major Chadwick, who was also visiting the ashram, adds, "The Swami entered that blissful state of meditation on the Infinite which is called samadhi. ...After giving darshan to Maugham in my room, Bhagavan returned to the Hall (while) the rest of the party remained in the room for tea. After tea, Somerset Maugham, who was wearing a large pair of boots, wanted to go to the Hall and see where Bhagavan usually lived. I took him to the western window through which he looked for some time with interest, making mental notes." There is one other brief account of Maugham's visit in *Talks with Sri Ramana Maharshi*, talk no. 550. That version concludes by saying: The author (Maugham) attempted to ask questions but did not speak. Major Chadwick encouraged him to ask. Sri Bhagavan said, "All finished. Heart talk is all talk. All talk must end in silence only."

Another famous visitor was Henri Cartier-Bresson, the celebrated Frenchman, who is regarded as a photographic genius. He arrived at Ramanasramam to record photographs of the great sage for posterity, just as Sri Bhagavan was approaching Mahasamadhi. These memorable photographs were later published in book form. Bresson also observed the miraculous event of a meteor moving towards Arunachala as Bhagavan left his body.

Of course, there were a great many notable visitors from many countries and all walks of life, who came in Sri Bhagavan's lifetime, ranging from devout monks of the Ramakrishna order to India's reigning maharajahs. Mahatma Gandhi also used to advise his close associates to visit the Maharshi whenever they needed recharging of their spiritual batteries.

However, while the visits of important personages are interesting to record, it is important to recognise the merits of the hosts of ordinary devoted men and women who came to see him and receive his darshan. Many later became close devotees and eventually, by practising his Teaching, attained Self-realisation. The author David Godman has recorded the memories of some of these close devotees in his masterly three-volume work *The Power of the Presence*.

We must necessarily now look at Sri Bhagavan's health during these closing years. As a *jivanmukta*, permanently established in the egoless state, it meant that he was fully surrendered in relation to any bodily ailments which might arise. He saw these temporary afflictions as if they were happening to someone else, as in a dream, because he was not identified with his physical form. Broadly speaking, he was a Naturopath who believed and recommended traditional herbal remedies, and he strongly advocated a strict vegetarian diet with milk products, to attain the necessary sattvic mind, which he said was a very great aid to Self-realisation.

At the close of 1948, however, a small growth appeared on his left elbow. It slowly grew in size and became somewhat painful. By February 1949, it was diagnosed as a cancerous tumour. After much protest, he eventually agreed to having it removed surgically. Regrettably, after this

*Henri Cartier-Bresson (inset) clicked while taking a picture of Sri Ramana's devotees.*

minor operation, the tumour returned. Eminent surgeons were summoned and said that the tumour was malignant and must be operated upon. It was later treated with radium, although sarcomatic. When an amputation was recommended, Bhagavan's comment was:

"There is no need for alarm. The body is itself a disease. Let it have its natural end. Why mutilate it? Simple dressing of the affected part is enough."

When the devotees prayed for Bhagavan's recovery, he was asked about the efficacy of their efforts. He replied with a smile:

"It is certainly desirable to be engaged in good activities; let them continue. Everything will come right in due course. Who is there to will this?" He quoted a verse in Sanskrit – "Let the body, the result of fructifying karma, rest or move about, live or die, the sage who has realised the Self is not aware of it, just as one in drunken stupor is not aware of his clothing."

Even during his final days, he continued to give darshan to the hundreds of devotees, reclining on his bed majestically. Two days before his Mahasamadhi, he gave an intensive gaze of grace to all those who passed before him. On April 14, 1950, hundreds of devotees gathered near his bedroom and began chanting his hymn to Arunachala, with the chorus *"Arunachala Shiva!"* From his eyes flowed tears of ecstasy. Then the last breaths followed smoothly, and finally stopped.

The onlookers saw a comet moving from south to north and then disappearing behind the peak of Arunachala. This phenomenon was noticed all over Southern India and reported worldwide in newspapers. Sri Bhagavan had moved into his reality, the Heart of the Universe. He had said,

"I am going away? Where could I go? I am here."

Today, most of his devotees know these words are literally true, and realise that their blessed Sri Bhagavan was not only his comely body, who dwelled at Arunachala for fifty-four years, but was actually the formless Absolute Pure Consciousness of *Sat Chit Ananda*, and as such lives eternally in the hearts of all his devotees who love him, and practise his Teaching.

This Supreme Guru, one of the greatest spiritual figures ever to grace our planet, had left his physical body but remained eternally in the hearts of all those who loved him, and as their *Satguru* (True master), they always continue to receive his guidance.

*Devotees pay homage and meditate at the samadhi of Sri Ramana Maharshi.*

*The road leading to the holy mountain of Arunachala.*

# Chapter Eleven

# THE IMPORTANCE OF ARUNACHALA TODAY

*"He who dedicates his mind to Thee, and seeing Thee, always beholds the universe as Thy figure, he who at all times glorifies Thee and loves Thee as none other than the Self, he is the master without rival, being one with Thee, and lost in Thy Bliss, O Arunachala!"*

– V. 5, Arunachala Pancharatna

There is no question that after Sri Bhagavan's Mahasamadhi, he soon became renowned as a Supreme Guru worldwide. Visitors and devotees still continued to flock to Sri Bhagavan's ashram at Arunachala even after his departure from the body. The reasons for this phenomenon are simple and straightforward. Firstly, Arunachala retains its reputation as a sacred Hill after millennia of pilgrimage and is considered a great Shiva linga, which exercises a tremendous spiritual power that is still experienced by the devotees who know it to be God, in the form of a mountain, just as their Master affirmed.

Secondly, Ramanasramam, so beautifully maintained and managed, retains his influence, and the subtle impressions of his presence may still be experienced there. This is true especially at his samadhi, the Mother's temple and in the old and new Halls, Skandasramam and the caves where he lived and taught. Thirdly, his Teaching has been clearly stated by him from every angle and perspective, and is easily practised in life without having to change one's status as a householder or one's lifestyle, whatever nationality one belongs to or whichever country in which one lives. His important innovation of bringing Self-Enquiry into the open has a tremendous appeal because, as he said, it is an infallible way to Self-realisation – the Direct Path.

Arunachala is a wondrous place of great, natural beauty and the emerald green environment is being restored with exquisite care. There is the judicious planting of many selected trees and shrubs, and the well-trodden paths are maintained and renewed. The caves and buildings are well looked after and preserved in all their sanctity. Beautiful bird and animal life abounds there. In coming to

Arunachala via Tiruvannamalai, a hospitable market town with its magnificent Shiva temple, still stands as one of the holiest in Southern India. Furthermore, Arunachala continues to hold out its Puranic promise for Self-realisation for all those who revere the Hill in their hearts. So, altogether, Arunachala, and the impeccable, miraculous life of Ramana Maharshi, with his great universal Teaching, still acts as a tremendous magnet attracting devotees in ever-increasing numbers from all over the world.

The ashram has grown to accommodate this influx of visitors by building more suitable accommodation and an enlarged dining hall. A new, aesthetically designed Archival Centre has been established for posterity to preserve all the known records of his life and Teaching. The ashram Library is a treasure house of extensive Upanishadic and Vedic literature, as well as the ever growing Ramana Maharshi literature which the ashram's book depot distributes and sells to all who come. There is a free dispensary offering medical treatment for visitors and dwellers in the locality.

As the great Tamil poet, Muruganar, Self-realised through Sri Bhagavan's grace, eloquently wrote in the invocation to his long poem on Sri Bhagavan's extensive Teaching, the *Garland of Guru's Sayings...*

"The ocean girdled maiden Earth's
Hard, long penance has borne fruit,
Pure being, glorious Shiva Himself,
Embodied in human form as Guru Ramana
Of flawless wisdom
Has come to us.
Let us in the heart
Cherish His sacred feet."

*An early view of Arunachaleswara Rajagorpuram and Arunachala.*

# IN PRAISE OF BHAGAVAN
# SRI RAMANA MAHARSHI

A free versification of the English prose translation from the Sanskrit, of *The Forty Verses in Praise of Sri Ramana* by Ganapati Muni.

*Boundless Bliss flooded the Heart of beauteous Mother Earth,*
*A sage came as Ramana to save us, he took a human birth.*

*Because the Lord of Mercy whose days on Arunachala Hill*
*Led a life of glory that ever shines and clears away all ill,*
*By his great realisation of that Everlasting Truth,*
*Revealed by Lord Krishna in his Bhagavad Gita forsooth:*
*Like Dakshinamurti in samadhi was shown to man by Shiva,*
*An emblem of silence, revealed to great sage Sanaka.*

*He's the revered Enlightened Master and gracious guide*
*Of all learned scholars with Ganapati at his side.*
*He's possessed of all the highest virtues known to man,*

*His radiant effulgence is manfully clad in body's plan*
*Of material sheaths, when weaved together make five in sum.*
*Behind dark worldly clouds he shines, a brilliant blazing Sun!*

*He's perfect as the ruler over those five senses so unruly,*
*He sees only merits in others, so clearly and so truly,*
*He ever abides in the blessed blissfulness of peace,*
*In his Being, pernicious poisoned passions have long ceased.*
*He lives only on the free offerings of caring devotees,*
*He dwells as an ascetic on hill slopes, ever there to please.*

*His Heart is proof against sharp arrows of carnal desire,*
*He's the living embodiment of Lord Agni's sacred fire!*
*He's devoted his days to teaching knowledge of Jnana,*
*He's crossed the stormy ocean of dreaded Samsara.*
*He uses his hands soft as a lotus to serve as a bowl,*
*Fear ends for souls taking refuge in Him to make themselves whole.*

*At his feet, by his intensive and most powerful gaze*
*His auspicious presence is felt as a fierce fiery blaze.*
*He crushes the load of devotee's dark misery to dust,*
*And scatters it along with latent tendencies of lust.*
*He's a safe haven of protection, security and peace,*
*His brightness of light chases away sorrow with ease.*

*His virtues are mirrored in rocks, streams and leaves,*
*His wise truthful words calm any soul who grieves.*
*He's never over elated by praise nor depressed by blame.*

He's foremost among all sages, world famous his name!
He's relentlessly cut off the despicable ego-mind,
He's overthrown all inner enemies that mankind finds.

Greed, anger, lust, jealousy, pride and infatuation,
He's immersed in a flood of blissful sublimation,
He's climbed the peak of mountainous transcendental height,
Through his own vision he's seen Divinity's dazzling light,
Well-nigh impossible for poor suffering ignorant others,
He's free from arrogance; he feels all men are brothers.

In ancient times he pierced Krauncha Hill like Skanda,
To forego joys of being fondled by his mother Uma,
That he might be reborn in human form as Sri Ramana,
To shatter dense spiritual darkness of Earth's samsara.
As an ascetic wearing only a clean loin cloth of white,
He rode on the back of a celestial peacock, fan-tail so bright.

He's now descended as a humble soul on dear Mother Earth,
To reign over the world, a Master unique in human birth.
Salutations to that One who transcends all attributes,
The celibate, with human skills and talents most astute.
The master and slayer of dark diabolical Taraka,
An emblem of man's dark ignorance, an arrogant Asura.

There's no divine peacock that can bear one of his ilk,
No Ganges he can bathe in, no nectar of mother's milk.
From the breasts of Goddess Parvati, no celestial choir

*Of veena players to sing and gently while away each hour.*
*Oh great pounder of Krauncha Hill! How do you still abide*
*On sacred heights of Arunachala, evermore to reside?*

*He's a God divine but sports only a single face,*
*He left his fond Mother Parvati's sacred place.*
*He doesn't wield a silver spear in his nimble hand,*
*He takes human form to deceive this sleeping land,*
*He hasn't celestial armies marching for him there,*
*Enough of this mask by which you bewitch the unaware!*

*But how will you escape your brother Ganapati's sight?*
*Some worship you as best among realised Rishi's bright,*
*Some as a Jnani, great Guru of gurus, beyond compare,*
*Others as an humble ascetic, wise, comely and fair.*
*But all of them prostrate before your sacred lotus feet,*
*Yet only two or three see you as Skanda, a God who's complete.*

*You explained the significance of Aum to great Lord Brahma,*
*You spoke to tell Truth to your father, sacred Lord Shiva.*
*You've kindly become the teacher of your elder brother*
*Ganapati, to whom you're beloved as his mother.*
*Subrahmanya you've outstripped your elders by such merit,*
*For generations to come, much sage wisdom they'll inherit!*

*The seat of honour reserved for those of most worth,*
*Once enjoyed by great sage Vyasa of high noble birth,*
*Later by dispeller of darkness saintly Lord Shankara,*

*Now awaits you, the Master sage, great Lord Ramana!*
*Commander-in-Chief of the celestial army's plan,*
*You've now come to planet Earth embodied as man.*

*Now when righteousness and religion seem at an end,*
*When all worlds are driven mad around sanity's bend,*
*And wretched scholars have lost sight of Ultimate Truth,*
*Disputing polemics; when even God's existence forsooth*
*Is disputed, who else can be our safe haven and refuge?*
*Oh Skanda born on Earth as man, save us from such deluge!*

*Though dispassion's crucial, can you withhold your grace replete?*
*Though effortlessness is desired, must worship of your holy Feet*
*Be condemned? Though desire's wholly contemptible for you,*
*Would that cause you to cease from guarding your sadhaks true?*
*Oh Skanda hidden in a handsome body with a human mask,*
*Why do you still bide your time? I most respectfully ask.*

*Away with empty dispute, discourse and discussion vain,*
*Righteousness! No longer need you walk or limp so maim,*
*Bewilderment and confusion will be wiped from the world,*
*Good shall flourish everywhere and Truth be unfurled!*
*Because our Lord, foremost of gurus, the son of Parvati*
*Was once incarnate on Earth with his brother Ganapati.*

*Oh mankind, revere this brother of Ganapati, the Master*
*Who's come in bodily form for now and forever after.*
*The Self, pervading the microcosm and the macrocosm,*

*Who is behind the souls of all, model of perfect altruism.*
*Source of the ego in which all weird difference is lost,*
*Who drags his children to moksha regardless of cost.*

*Hail Bhagavan Ramana Maharshi, Universal Master!*
*Dispeller of misery from this sad world ever after,*
*Who chases away darkness from his dear devotees,*
*As pure eternal Consciousness ever ready to please,*
*Abiding in the heart, blazing bright within and without,*
*Bereft of the least trace of ignorance, with none left to Doubt.*

*Self's the transcendental Truth that's underlying*
*The world and beyond, there can be no denying.*
*Oh Ramana, pray turn your gracious glance my way,*
*So that I may be eternally blest, forever on this day.*
*Oh Bhagavan, you're the Jagadguru of all mankind,*
*Your boundless heart knows no differences, so I find.*

*Troubled world, egotism and God are now all observed,*
*As one transcendental Reality by virtue of your word.*
*The recalcitrant wicked ego has been struck down to die,*
*I now exist as that One Reality which isn't apart from "I".*
*By your Grace our hearts readily realise the Divine Self,*
*Hidden within the perverted mind, that vile demonic elf.*

*Blessedness isn't a virtue for you, oh prince of sages!*
*Its natural in your shining heart you've known for ages,*
*Oh spotless Being your form blazes with effulgent light,*

*Infinite is your penetrating gaze, so brilliant and bright.*
*Oh Lord your egotistic mind has vanished in your Heart,*
*You dwell in eternal Sat Chit Ananda, never to depart!*

*You're the acknowledged chief among ascetics severe,*
*You've been deputed to roast Souls for the Lord who is near,*
*You chop off egos and well season them for tasty food.*
*I worship and revere you, who does each deed for good.*
*You pierce through our ignorance dwelling in the heart,*
*By virtue of your grace, and piercing glance you will to impart.*

*You're beatific, but your poor devotees are of little worth,*
*Thrown headlong into a sea of uncertain death and rebirth,*
*Being drowned in their worldly desires without respite,*
*And falling endlessly exhausted every noon and night.*
*They reach for the two lily flowers afloat in mid-sea,*
*And clutch for safety at your lotus feet most earnestly.*

*Merciful Lord, grant the poor refugees your gaze to save;*
*You're so fearless, all powerful, grave, strong and brave.*
*If unsuckled by his mother, what's a babe's sad fate?*
*Where's safety for sheep when their good shepherd's irate?*
*Where's help for the soul pitched against God's mighty wrath?*
*How will ignorant ones conquer mind, as flame is to moth?*

*Master! Why not save the devotees pining at your feet?*
*Perfect peace spreads when you shower nectar so sweet,*
*By the lucid lunar-like smile that shines on your face,*

*Your steady gazing eyes grant incomparable grace,*
*Oh Lord, your pearl of silence is a gift of priceless worth,*
*It's unparalleled, oh Bhagavan, on this poor planet Earth.*

*The light of Parvati shines through your penetrating eyes,*
*Dispelling ignorant darkness that clouds the mind's skies.*
*Your face gleams with the grace and brilliance of Lakshmi,*
*Your words contain the secretive lore of goddess Saraswati,*
*Preceptor of the worlds, Sri Bhagavan Ramana the Great,*
*How can mere mortals praise the glory of your Realised state?*

*Good fortune visited the red mountain Arunachala,*
*For having sheltered great sages in the past, oh Ramana,*
*But now has grown unique because you've chosen this Hill,*
*Among many sacred places, there for your mission to fulfil.*
*Boundless bliss has flooded the heart of beauteous Mother Earth,*
*A sage came as Ramana to save us, he took a human birth!*

– Alan Jacobs

# SRI RAMANA MAHARSHI'S
# KEY TEACHINGS

The keystone of the Maharshi's Teaching is his Self-Enquiry or Atma Vichara, his infallible Direct Path to Self-realisation, coupled with total devotional surrender to God, Self or Guru.

Broadly speaking, Sri Bhagavan tells us that the immortal Self of Sat Chit Ananda or pure Existence-Consciousness-Awareness-Bliss is already there inherent in each of us. The difficulty is we do not recognise 'That', our true nature, or essential 'I Amness', because it is veiled and obscured by many latent tendencies and habits of the egotistic mind, which act as a mirror, and project a dream of the world, the body and the mind. Our identification with the mind and body is the chief reason for our failure to know ourself as we really are. Through persistent Self-Enquiry, devotion, and surrender of the egotistic mind to God or the Satguru in the Spiritual Heart, this obscuration and identification is gradually and gracefully removed, until the immortal Self is Realised. That is the full power of

*The Supreme Guru – Sri Ramana Maharshi.*

Absolute Consciousness and is known; the world is seen as Real because the substrate is perceived to be as Brahman.

I composed a 'Crown of Sonnets' sequence which was published in the *Mountain Path* some time ago, and gives his key Teaching in poetic form, as is customary in Tamil literature, thereby preserving their essential *rasa* or beauty.

## SRI RAMANA CORONA

*All beings yearn to be happy, always;*
*Happiness without a whinge of sorrow,*
*To enjoy a life of carefree days,*
*Taking no tinge of thought for tomorrow.*
*When restless mind's at peace in deep sleep,*
*What glimpse of worry, grief or despair?*
*So happiness lies therein, buried down deep.*
*How to find that treasure, awake, aware?*
*Ask the question, 'Who am I', from where?*
*That's the essential means of the holy task,*
*Ending ego's 'me' and 'my', that's there.*
*No pleasure endures in things on this earth,*
*Enquire within, who basks behind the mask?*
*To regain that Selfhood we lost at birth.*

*To regain that Selfhood we lost at birth,*
*First consider well the cinema screen.*
*To understand that, gains merit and worth.*
*On the screen there appears a tense drama,*
*The film begins and we enjoy the show.*
*Fire, flood, sex, death, a vast panorama;*
*The screen's unchanging, but the film's a shadow.*
*The simile teaches, strange as it may be,*

*That both seer and seen make up the mind.*
*On Consciousness as screen, all action's based.*
*The world's like a dream projected by mind*
*To know that is true, is the clue to be free,*
*A guiding beacon that's so rare to find.*
*That's the sage's wisdom by which we are graced.*

*That's the sage wisdom by which we are graced,*
*We're taught the silver screen as a metaphor.*
*Seated in theatre stalls, now we're placed,*
*To proceed with clarity and enquire some more.*
*The bright theatre lamp is the light supreme,*
*Illuminating both actors and the scene.*
*We see stage and the play only by light,*
*Yet when action ends, the lamp remains bright.*
*Just as woven cloth and its colour white*
*Are never, ever perceived as apart,*
*So when mind and light both unite,*
*They form ego, knotted and bound in the heart.*
*Of all that we've ever learned since birth,*
*That's the highest wisdom proclaimed on earth.*

*That's the highest wisdom proclaimed on earth,*
*How to make mind to merge in its source?*
*Only by enquiring with all of one's force,*
*The central question regarding its birth,*
*The ultimate scrutiny of 'Who Am I'?*
*As thoughts froth forth like waves on the ocean,*
*They'll all be slain by such introspection,*
*Unveiling the Self, the lost inward eye.*
*Pearls lay buried on the deep ocean floor,*
*Attracting divers to search for this goal.*
*Holding their breath they plunge to the core*
*Of the ocean bed, for the pearl oyster's soul.*
*To gain this gem in the heart's sacred place,*
*Just seek for the source where mind is based.*

*Just seek for the source where mind is based.*
*You travel alone on a mystery train;*
*By this metaphor we're comfortably placed,*
*To travel by providence free from pain.*
*So stack all that heavy baggage on the rack,*
*Only a fool carries it on his head!*
*Be glad, accept the predestined track,*
*Rest quietly, safe at home on your bed!*
*Surrender in joyful jubilation!*
*Surrender utterly to God's almighty will,*
*Surrender with total resignation,*
*Surrender knowing all will be well,*
*Surrender whole heartedly with one accord,*
*Take safe refuge in the all loving Lord!*

*Take safe refuge in the all loving Lord!*
*For life's a dream and sleeping dreams are short,*
*The waking dream is long; both stem from thought.*
*The Real is beyond both this waking and sleep.*
*The sword of enquiry slays dream states deep,*
*So reaching their substratum numinous,*
*The state of pure consciousness, Self luminous!*
*Blissfully aware, yet awake in sleep.*
*As the cockerel crows ready to sup,*
*At the roseate dawn of first morning light,*
*Awareness pours into the near empty cup,*
*Granting a moment's taste of Self insight.*
*This light is the eye that forever sees,*
*Who can be known by enquiring 'who frees?'*

*Who can be known by enquiring 'who frees?'*
*The Master who lives in the cave of the heart,*
*Not separate from one's Self, being the start,*
*Of the final search from bond to release.*
*The sage appears when the soul is ready,*

*With strong gaze of grace he says "Be aware*
*that God and his wisdom are already there!"*
*He acts as a brake to make the mind steady,*
*While mercy flows freely in sunshine and air,*
*Hindered only by our being unready.*
*If you come to Him, meekly with an empty cup,*
*His grace is then bound to fill it up.*
*The Master's glance is the grace of the Lord,*
*He cuts you free with His mighty sword.*

*He cuts you free with His mighty sword,*
*To guide you surely, on the upward way*
*To Self-realisation, your real birthday!*
*Consummation of 'That', the sage's word,*
*Is "rest in the Self," which is always heard.*
*In him, place great trust, affirm, say 'yea*
*As certainty'! Our Real Self blazes away,*
*Ever surrendered to the almighty Lord,*
*Revealing great peace for Realisation's sake,*
*Renouncing belief that a rope is a snake.*
*The seeker surely becomes 'the great find',*
*His own blissful being, the summit in kind,*
*This great Teaching eternally frees,*
*One with the Self, as the Absolute sees.*

*One with the Self, as the Absolute sees,*
*He answers all our prayers and our pleas;*
*We must first enter that dear sacred part,*
*Not the fleshy pump that throbs on the left,*
*But the sacred core: by being skilful and deft,*
*We find that on the right is the real Heart!*
*By harnessing breath, being adept and bright,*
*We dive with great skill and all of our might.*
*There dwelling in depths of our true heart's cave,*

*Lives the shining 'Unity' blazing as Self,*
*Pulsation of I-I, where all shadows cease.*
*So fixing gaze there, finally, off we stave,*
*Perverted, wandering, demonic mind elf,*
*Returning to 'Self', our birthright of peace.*

*Returning to 'Self', our birthright of peace,*
*Is knowing that all this vile body performs,*
*Was predestined before it ever took form.*
*So from stress, despair and fretting, please cease!*
*Our freedom dwells in our natural state,*
*Renouncing the 'I Am The Doer' notion,*
*Detached from fruit of form's puppet motion,*
*Yet grace can avert even predestined fate!*
*Be like a skilled actor on this stage of strife!*
*Play with goodwill the part you've been given,*
*No matter how strangely you find you are driven,*
*Knowing who, truly you are, in this life.*
*Until fate pulls down the final curtain,*
*Know you're Self not body, know that is certain!*

*Know you're Self not body, know that is certain!*
*In this Realisation, there's no cause to leave home,*
*You can strive in the city, there's no need to roam.*
*To change style of life would all be in vain,*
*For mind remains with you, until it is slain.*
*Demonic ghost ego, source and fabric of thought*
*Creates body and world, whereby we are caught.*
*Change of place, never changed the way we behave,*
*Whether living at home, in a forest or cave.*
*There are two ways by which our bonds may be freed:*
*Either ask "to whom is this strange fate decreed?"*
*Or surrender false 'me' to be then stricken down,*
*So praying intensely for 'my will' to cease,*
*We leave it to grace, to grant us release.*

*We leave it to grace, to grant us release.*
*God will do this through the gaze of his sage,*
*He sends down His messenger for every age,*
*To those who yearn and pray for great peace.*
*The realised sage lives on here and now,*
*Ever abiding as Self unclouded by the mind.*
*Humble, compassionate, loving and kind,*
*Wisely profound, as his way clearly shows.*
*He steers the vessel of firm devotees,*
*Fulfilling everyone's spiritual need.*
*In deep silence, he sits, with perfect ease,*
*To awaken those, whom his Teaching well heed.*
*Graciously, his great glance of initiation,*
*Drives the mind inwards, to Self-realisation!*

*Driving the mind inwards, to Self-realisation,*
*He grants safe passage through life's stormy ocean;*
*What frail soul will ever be excluded*
*From the presence of the holy Supreme?*
*No matter how depraved or deluded,*
*His mercy never ends, and will always redeem,*
*Raising the soul from the depth of depression,*
*To free one from the 'I am this body' obsession.*
*From passions that churn desire and aversion,*
*His fair breeze wafts clear equanimity;*
*Enmeshed no more in worldly adversity,*
*Never perturbed by praise nor foul enmity,*
*We learn that there's the greatest giving*
*In knowing all are Self, and so truly living.*

*In knowing all are Self, and so truly living,*
*We thank the great sage who is ever giving.*
*We praise the Lord, who leads us to His feet,*
*His gracious gaze is eternally sweet,*
*Without ceasing, he's forever reviving,*

*He grants that freedom, our real surviving.*
*He severs the grip of bondage's chains,*
*He frees the soul, where confusion reigns,*
*He bestows both compassion and deep peace,*
*He sends out his grace to grant us release.*
*He teaches the truth that Consciousness is all,*
*And Self-Enquiry to raise us up from our fall.*
*We praise God almighty who is ever living,*
*This crown of my verses is our thanksgiving!*

*To regain that Selfhood we lost from birth,*
*That's the sage wisdom by which we are graced,*
*This is the highest wisdom proclaimed on earth.*
*Just seek for the source where mind is based.*
*Take refuge in the all loving Lord,*
*Who can be known by enquiring 'who frees?'*
*He cuts you loose with his mighty sword,*
*One with the Self, as the Absolute sees.*
*Returning to Self, our birthright of peace,*
*Know you're Self, not body, know that is certain!*
*We leave it to grace, to grant us release.*
*He drives the mind inwards, to Self-realisation,*
*In knowing all are Self, and so truly living,*
*This crown of my verses is our thanksgiving!*

– Alan Jacobs

The 'shuddha satva' white peacock.

Appendix Three

# THE 'SHUDDHA SATVA' PEACOCK

One day in the April of 1947, a white peacock was presented to the ashram as a gift for Sri Ramana Maharshi from the Rani of Baroda. At first, the Maharshi thought it wise to send it back as he said, "Isn't it enough that ten or twelve coloured peacocks are here? They may come to fight with this one because it is of a different variety ... it is better to send it back to its own place."

However, the person who brought the white peacock just left it there and went away. Once, this peacock ran away somewhere and Krishnaswami, who had been deputed to its care, caught and brought it back. Sri Ramana placed one hand on its neck and with his other hand kept stroking the peacock up to its heart, admonishing it gently, "You naughty chap, where did you go? How can we manage to look after you if you go away like this? ... Why not stay on here?"

From then on, the white peacock would just wander around,

and sometimes into, the cottages within the ashram compound. One afternoon, the peacock was seen sitting by the side of a radio in one of the cottages, with its eyes closed as if in *dhyana* or meditation. Someone commented that the peacock was listening very attentively to the music. The Maharshi said, "The peacocks are very fond of music, especially if it is from the flute." Then someone said that though this peacock was white, the others peacocks were really more beautiful.

Sri Ramana said, "Those peacocks have beautiful colours but this one has a beauty of its own. This is pure white without the mixture of any other colours. That means it is *shuddha satva* – the pure self – without the mixture of other *gunas* or attributes. See, in Vedantic language, the peacock also can be taken as an example. Even other peacocks do not have so many colours at birth. They have only one colour. As they grow up, they get many colours. When their tails grow, they have any number of eyes. See how many colours and how many eyes! Our mind is also like that. At birth, there are no perversities. Subsequently, there will be many activities and ideas, like the colours of the peacock."

Many devotees had observed that this white peacock was the reincarnation of Madhava swami, who had been one of Sri Ramana's long-serving attendants who had passed away a year before on the 12th of July, 1946. Whenever the white peacock came into the hall, it would make a point of inspecting the books on the shelves, which used to be one of Madhava swami's duties. The peacock would often peck at the books that Madhava swami had repaired and rebound, but not touch any of the other books. Further, when Madhava swami was alive, he would always sit on a concrete bench near the door. Now, the white peacock would come and sit on the bench that the swami sat on.

Sri Ramana would himself occasionally address the peacock fondly as 'Madhava'. G. V. Subbaramayya in his book *Sri Ramana Reminiscences* writes, "On June 20, 1947, I composed eight Telugu verses on the white peacock in *mayura vrittam* – the peacock metre, and presented them to Sri Bhagavan in the Jubilee pandal. He appeared greatly pleased with them and handing them to Srimati Lalita Venkataraman, he suggested that she might sing them with her veena. Within half an hour, she brought her veena and got ready to sing. Just then the white peacock was absent. Sri Bhagavan said, 'But the hero must be present to hear his praises sung! Where are you, Madhava? Come.'

"Lo! At once, the white peacock jumped down from the roof of the pandal; and while Lalita Venkataraman sang, he spread out his tail feathers and danced, as Sri Bhagavan sat and watched him with beaming eyes. When the singing concluded, the peacock walked to the veena and pecked at its strings with his beak. Thereupon, Sri Bhagavan told the singer, 'Madhava wants you to repeat the song.' So she sang once more and the peacock danced again. It was a sight for the gods to see."

Source: *Saranagathi* – eNewsletter www.sriramanamaharshi.org, January 2010, Vol. 4, Issue 1, *Letters from Sri Ramanasramam* by Suri Nagamma, *Sri Ramana Reminiscences* by G. V. Subbaramayya.

*A picture of the main entrance to Ramanasramam in the early days.*

Appendix Four

# ACTIVITIES IN THE ASHRAM

Bhagavan's samadhi is the focus of daily pujas and the venue of celebrations, chanting, meditation, worship and gatherings during special occasions and festivals.

The Mother's temple is a place for worship, meditation and occasional pujas.

The old Hall is maintained as a place of silent meditation.

The Book Store contains an extensive stock of the Ramana literature with over sixty titles, CDs, DVDs, souvenirs and photographs. Also on sale are the principal Advaita Classics recommended by the Maharshi, as well as the famed ashram monthly magazine the *Mountain Path*.

The path to Skandasramam is well-maintained, enabling devotees to climb Arunachala as far and as high as they safely wish.

The Pradakshina route is clearly marked out and maps are available.

### Goshala

One can visit the ashram's Dairy and Cattle Farm where a fine herd of cows provide dairy products for use in the kitchen.

### Vedapathshala

A *Yajurveda** school where young students of the Vedas are trained for this traditional vocation leading to priesthood, and where they chant daily for pujas and the Sanskrit *Vedaparayanas* (recitations of Vedic texts).

There are afternoon readings from selected Ramana literature in Tamil and English.

### Library

The Sri Ramana Centenary Library houses over 30,000 volumes and current periodicals in various languages, and are available for guests.

### Dispensary

There is free medical attention for guests, residents and the local population.

### Arunachaleswar

The magnificent Shiva temple at the heart of the market town of Tiruvannamalai is open for visitors, pujas and festivals.

---

* One of the four Vedas, the Yajurveda contains the liturgy (mantras) needed to perform the sacrifices of the religion of the Vedic period.

**Daily Routine**

The day begins early and follows a set routine:

6:45 am  –  Milk Offering. Followed by Breakfast.

8:00 am  –  Sanskrit Vedaparayana

10:00 am  –  Morning Puja

11:30 am  –  Lunch

4:00 pm  –  Tea or Tamil Group Reading

4:30 pm  –  English Group Reading

5:00 pm  –  Sanskrit Vedaparayana

6:15 pm  –  Evening Puja

6:30 pm  –  Tamil Parayana

7:30 pm  –  Supper

*The Ramanasramam as it is today at Tiruvannamalai, Tamil Nadu.*

# RAMANA CENTRES IN INDIA
# AND ABROAD

## INDIA

Sri Ramanasramam, Tiruvannamalai, Tamil Nadu. +91-4175-237200

Sri Sundaram Mandiram, Tiruchuzhi, Tamil Nadu. +91-4566-282217

Sri Ramana Mandiram, Madurai, Tamil Nadu. +91-452-2346102

Sri Ramana Mandiram, Desur, Tamil Nadu.

Sri Ramana Kendra, Mylapore, Chennai, Tamil Nadu. +91-44-24611397

Sri Ramana Kendram, Hyderabad, Andhra Pradesh. +91-40-27424092

Sri Ramana Kendra, New Delhi. +91-11-24626997

RMCL, Bangalore, Karnataka. +91-80-23360799, 23512639

## MAURITIUS

Sri Ramana Maharshi Centre, Reduit, Mauritius. +230-4640823

## NORTH AMERICA

Ann Arbor MI, USA. +1 (734)-623-7199

Arunachala Ashrama NYC, NY, USA. +1 (718)-560-3196

Atlanta GA, USA. +1 (678)-546-0378

Dublin OH, USA. +1 (614)-348-1975

East Lyme CT, USA. +1 (860)-691-1862

F. Lauderdale FL, USA. +1 (954)-755-4758

Goshen IN, USA. +1 (574)-875-6298

Los Angeles CA, USA. +1 (310)-473-9441

San Jose CA, USA. +1 (510)-656-2752

Santa Fe, New Mexico, USA. +1 (858)-922-6476

SAT (Society of Abidance in Truth) NC, USA. +1 (831)-425-7287

Arunachala Ashrama, Nova Scotia, Canada. +1 (902)-665-2090

Ottawa ON, Canada. +1 (713)-733-8250

Toronto ON, Canada. +1 (905)-849-6005

**EUROPE**

London, UK. +44 (0)-020 8398 0193

**AUSTRALIA**

Sydney, Australia.

# BIBLIOGRAPHY

*Self-Realisation* by B. V. Narasimha Swami

*Arunachala Ramana, Boundless Ocean of Grace*
by Capt. Narayan, 8 Volumes

*Sri Maharshi: A Short Life Sketch,* by M. S. Kamath

*Ramana Maharshi: A Life,* by Gabriele Ebert

*Sadhu's Reminiscences of Ramana Maharshi,*
by Sadhu Arunachala (Major A. W. Chadwick)

*Living By The Words of Bhagavan,* by David Godman

*The Power of the Presence,* by David Godman, 3 Volumes

*Letters from Sri Ramanasramam,* by Suri Nagamma

*A Practical Guide to Know Yourself and Conversations with
Sri Ramana Maharshi,* by A. R. Natarajan

*Talks with Ramana Maharshi*
Collected Works of Ramana Maharshi

*Talks with Ramana Maharshi:*
*On Realizing Abiding Peace and Happiness*

*Guru Ramana,* by S. S. Cohen

*Moments Remembered: Reminiscences of Bhagavan Ramana,*
by V. Ganesan

*Living with the Master,* Reminiscences by Kunjuswami

*Sri Ramana Reminiscences,* by G. V. Subbaramayya

*Face To Face With Sri Ramana Maharshi*
Compiled by Professor Laxmi Narain

*Five Hymns to Sri Arunachala,* by Sri Ramana Maharshi

All these books and many others are available from
Sri Ramanasramam Book Depot.

# ACKNOWLEDGEMENTS

To Shri V. S. Ramanan, President of Ramanasramam, for graciously granting permission to use copyright material from the Ramana Maharshi literature for inclusion in this Biography.

To Gautam Sachdeva, for suggesting such a Biography, and all his helpful suggestions.

To John Maynard and other members of the Sri Ramanasramam Archival Centre for researching and supplying the necessary photographs to illustrate this book.

To Shiv Sharma, for his editorial and design assistance.

The publisher gratefully acknowledges the generous support of Dev Varyani for this project.

For further details, contact:
Yogi Impressions Books Pvt. Ltd.
1711, Centre 1, World Trade Centre,
Cuffe Parade, Mumbai 400 005, India.

Fill in the Mailing List form on our website
and receive, via email, information on
books, authors, events and more.
Visit: www.yogiimpressions.com

Telephone: (022) 61541500, 61541541
E-mail: yogi@yogiimpressions.com

 Join us on Facebook:
www.facebook.com/yogiimpressions

Printed in Great Britain
by Amazon

33209343R00089